Booktalks, Bookwalks, and Read-Alouds

Booktalks, Bookwalks, and Read-Alouds

Promoting the Best New Children's Literature Across the Elementary Curriculum

Rosanne J. Blass

2002
LIBRARIES UNLIMITED
Teacher Ideas Press
A Division of Greenwood Publishing Group, Inc.
Westport, Connecticut

LIBRARIES UNLIMITED
Teacher Ideas Press
A Division of Greenwood Publishing Group, Inc.
88 Post Road West
Westport, CT 06881
1-800-225-5800
www.lu.com

ISBN 1-56308-810-X

Contents

Introduction

The importance of reading and books in the life of a child cannot be underestimated. Reading may be the single most important skill needed for a child's educational success and also can be one of the most enjoyable experiences in childhood. Books transport readers beyond the immediacy of time and place into the past as it was or might have been, into the future as it might be, and from here to far-away realms of fact and fantasy. Books introduce us to new characters, teach us important life lessons, help us understand ourselves and others, and inspire us.

Reading builds literacy. As literacy grows, so do language and conceptual development until reading and writing become the tools of empowerment and possibility, the tools by which the reader achieves academic success and satisfying life experiences. An appreciation for books and a desire to read begin with the home and family, continue in school, and are supported by the community and social relationships. This guide is designed to help educators foster an appreciation of and interest in books and to link reading to curriculum studies.

Building a collection and creating access to literature are only the first steps of this endeavor. By sharing their enthusiasm about and interest in books, parents and educators communicate the message that reading is something to get excited about. For many years, librarians and media specialists have used booktalks to promote their collections. Booktalks are short promotional presentations designed to entice readers into reading particular books. Until recently, booktalks have been used mostly with older readers—teens and adults—but even young children will respond to this type of book promotion. Modifying the approach of traditional booktalks to fit the needs of young readers is an effective tool for reading promotion. This book is one of the few resources available that provides booktalks for young readers.

The books chosen for inclusion in this guide represent some of the best new publications in children's literature. Titles were selected from those reviewed and recommended by publications such as: *Booklist, Book Report, Book Talks, Bulletin of the Center for Children's Books, JOYS, School Library Journal, VOYA: Voices of Youth Advocates, Wilson Bulletin,* and *Reading Teacher*. Selections include many award-winning books and authors, as well as books that represent emerging trends in children's literature. Emphasis is on new releases, that is, books published from 1998 to 2001, with representative titles of both fiction and nonfiction for elementary and middle school children.

In short, you'll find a wide assortment of books that appeal to the variety of young readers in the elementary grades—traditional and nontraditional (intended for fluent rather than beginning readers) picture books, alphabet books, concept books, early readers, easy chapter books, novellas, junior novels, biographies and autobiographies, poetry, short stories, humor, riddles, and puzzles.

The booktalks are organized by curriculum area because with this age group reading is often done within the parameters of school subjects. Of course, the links in these books are not limited to a single subject area. Most can be used across the curriculum, and you'll see that the curriculum connections often include suggestions for other subject areas. However, by placing titles within a subject area, educators can more easily use these books to enhance curricular studies. Likewise, students will be encouraged to make learning connections with their reading.

The four chapters are based on standard elementary school curriculum areas: language arts and literature, mathematics and science, social studies, and arts and recreation. Each entry provides bibliographic information, age level, a book summary, a booktalk (or instructions for a bookwalk or read-aloud), curriculum connections, and identification of related books for further reading. Titles appropriate for speakers of English as a second language are noted by the abbreviation ESOL. Age levels are generally based on publishers' recommendations, but in some cases modifications were made based on the ease or difficulty of the language used and concepts developed. Parents and educators are urged to use these levels only as a general guide and to use their own judgment in selecting titles. Curriculum connections given with each title can help educators connect reading activities to other school studies. (All websites were accessed on June 15, 2002.) They are intended to stimulate ideas and learning extensions, rather than to give full, detailed activity directions, although sample graphic organizers, directions, and recipes are included in the appendixes. Educators and parents will need to adapt these ideas to fit the needs of the children with whom they are working.

The primary audience for this book consists of public librarians, school librarians, and media specialists who work with elementary-grade children, but teachers and parents will also find the book eminently useful. Public librarians who serve young students in the library or who make school visits can use these booktalks to promote their collection and services. School library media specialists will find the booktalks valuable in selecting and promoting books in classrooms and in the media center. They may also want to refer to this book when making selections for purchase. Classroom and reading teachers, curriculum specialists, church educators, and home-school parents and teachers might use the guide to identify books for read-alouds or to identify books that complement specific topics they are covering in class.

Tips and Guidelines for Booktalking with Young Readers

When working with young children, it is important to be interactive and to encourage participation. Show the book to the children as you tell them about it. Ask the children questions, and listen to their responses. In some cases, you may want to have children repeat specific phrases from your booktalk. You also can do a bookwalk as you speak. While talking, take your young listeners for a "walk" through the book by turning the pages and showing the pictures. Make a point of using the language and vocabulary of the book so that it becomes familiar to the children as they listen.

With very young learners and for simple picture books, you are encouraged to read the story aloud. Get into the story and let your natural expressiveness emerge. Be sure to occasionally make eye contact with your audience. A spirited first reading with beginning readers can often prompt multiple successive readings.

When selecting titles for your booktalk, be sure to read them first. Choose books that you enjoy and that you think the children will also enjoy. You should also have multiple copies of the books that you booktalk because the children will want to read the book right away.

The booktalks in this guide are meant as templates only. There is no need to memorize them word for word. You can and should adapt them to your own style and to fit your own purposes. Never read a booktalk. Instead, make the booktalks your own by using your own "voice" and wording.

Children's Literature Today

The books chosen for this guide reflect some of the recent trends in publishing. These books lend themselves to curricular applications. It is easy to see how books that celebrate creation and the environment, as exemplified by Brian Patten's *The Blue & Green Ark* and Joe Miller's *If the Earth . . . Were a Few Feet in Diameter*, can be used in the study of nature and science. The many creative retellings of fairy tales and folktales, including cultural variations, fractured tales, and extensions of familiar tales, provide fine springboards to creative writing and story-telling exercises. The resurgence of fantasy books is a boon to educators encouraging creative thinking, and the proliferation of accurate and engaging historical fiction makes history come alive for readers. Some of the recurring themes and topics of historical fiction and nonfiction are stories of World War II, immigrants in the 1900s, and life in the twentieth century. In these books, young readers can meet personalities such as Amelia Bloomer (suffragist), Princess Ka'iulani (Hawaii's last princess), Sarah Forbes Benetta (African Princess), and many others.

Nontraditional picture books are intended to appeal to fluent rather than beginning readers. Lynn Curlee's three books, *Rushmore*, *Liberty*, and *Brooklyn Bridge,* recount the engineering feats that made possible the carving of Mount Rushmore and the building of the Statue of Liberty and the Brooklyn Bridge. *Molly Bannaky* tells the story of the English milkmaid, banished to the New World as an indentured servant, who became Benjamin Bennicker's grandmother.

Eve Bunting's *The Butterfly House* and Andrea Spalding and Janet Wilson's *Me and Mr. Mah* are examples of the growing number of intergenerational stories, which are often ideal for social studies lessons.

The influence of technology becomes apparent in computer-generated illustrations, such as those used by David Kirk in *Nova's Ark* and by Jane Wattenberg in *Henny-Penny*. These books can stimulate young minds in new ways. Multi-tasking comes to children's books as evidenced by the combination of readable text, rich illustrations, sidebars, running time lines, dialogue balloons, charts, and diagrams. Two examples are Peter Sis's *Starry Messenger: Galileo Galilei* and The Magic School Bus Series by Joanna Cole and Bruce Degen.

Examples of exciting illustrations include the lavish use of gold leaf by Leo and Diane Dillon in Virginia Hamilton's *The Girl Who Spun Gold* and by Demi in *The Emperor's New Clothes*. Authentic representations of late-eighteenth-century France can be found in Diane Goode's *The Dinosaur's New Clothes* and *Cinderella the Dog and Her Little Glass Slipper*. Baba Waque Diakite uses vibrant, ceramic-tile paintings bordered by a black-and-white monkey motif that was popular in European art during and after the Middle Ages in his retelling of the West African folktale, *The Hatseller and the Monkeys*. Isaac O. Olaleye illustrates his retelling of a Nigerian folktale with vibrant collages. This wonderful array of illustrative styles and media may inspire young readers to pursue their own artistic creations.

The trends in children's publishing, whether in theme, style, or format and presentation, are truly exciting. They offer great promise to today's and tomorrow's readers. It is my hope that you and your students will find many books to enjoy, share, and learn from within this guide. Happy reading!

CHAPTER 1

Language Arts and Literature

INTRODUCTION

Virtually any book can be used to enhance language arts and literature. Trade books are natural and vital complements to language arts study, and some are especially suited to this purpose. Alphabet books can make a potentially dull subject come alive for young learners. Fantasy and adventure stories stimulate young imaginations while introducing children to the elements of story. Retellings of familiar folktales and fairy tales reiterate story elements and can easily prompt writing responses. Mysteries are also very popular with children. In addition to enhancing language arts and reading comprehension, they can be used to encourage problem solving and critical thinking skills. Children's poetry introduces young readers to the delights of language and leads naturally into writing projects. Short stories, humor, riddles, and puzzles can tickle a child's mind and prompt a multitude of creative responses.

ALPHABET BOOKS

Azarian, Mary. **A Gardener's Alphabet**. Boston: Houghton Mifflin, 2000. Unpaged. $16.00. ISBN 0-618-03380-7.

- **PICTURE BOOK—ESOL**
- **AGES 5–8**

Summary

Bold, colorful, detailed woodcuts illustrate the one-word or one-phrase text in this alphabet book that opens the world of gardens and gardening to readers of all ages.

Booktalk/Bookwalk

Let's step into the garden and begin by reading together in the arbor. You can plant bulbs, make compost, dig a garden bed, and then put your tools away in a shed that holds everything. Cool your feet in the fountain, water plants in the greenhouse, harvest pumpkins, and watch insects on the vines. Or visit a Japanese garden or a kitchen garden, set out lawn ornaments, and spread manure. Chase away the animals that are nibbling in the vegetable garden, walk through the ornamental grasses, prune the branches, and pick Queen Anne's lace. Now it's time for a rest in the hammock after which you'll plant seeds and trim a topiary. Oh, look at what's happening underground! What do you see? (Stop here to have children identify objects in the picture.) Above ground you can see the vegetables. Now it's time to weed the flower beds. Finally you will visit a Xeriscape garden, then a yard, and finish by carrying a great big zucchini.

Curriculum Connections

Richly detailed illustrations lend themselves to conversations about the word meanings and concepts that are introduced on each page. Not quite a wordless book, this alphabet book can be used to develop oral and written language. It is also likely to appeal to and be appropriate for use with children who are English speakers of other languages (ESOL).

Related Books

Other books by Mary Azarian are *A Farmer's Alphabet* and *Snowflake Bentley*. Use these books in conjunction with the study of the art form of woodblocks.

Horenstein, Henry. **Arf! Beg! Catch! Dogs from A to Z.** New York: Scholastic Press, 1999. Unpaged. $12.95. ISBN 0-590-03380-8.

■ **PICTURE BOOK—ESOL**
■ **AGES 3–6**

Summary

Realistic, color photographs of different breeds of dogs illustrate the pages that introduce both the capital and small letters of the alphabet and one word that identifies the action or describes an aspect of the photograph. Although intended for young readers, ages 3–6, the photographs are likely to appeal to readers of all ages.

Bookwalk

Read aloud and on each page point first to the letter, then to the word as you say, "A is for Arf!" Encourage children to chime in with "A is for Arf!"

Curriculum Connections

Use this book for shared and repeated readings. Use the colorful alphabet at the end of the book to review letter names. Encourage children to name their own words that begin with the letters. Finally, talk about the dog photos on the last two pages. Ask children to identify a letter of the alphabet and a word that begins with that letter to accompany each photo. This book would also be appropriate to use with children who are English speakers of other languages (ESOL).

Patten, Brian. **The Blue & Green Ark**. New York: Scholastic Press, 1999. Unpaged. Illustrated by David Armitage, Sian Bailey, Patrick Benson, Tim Clarey, Jason Cockcroft, Cathie Felstead, Karin Littlewood, Nick Maland, David Parkins, Jane Ray, and Helen Ward. $18.95. ISBN 0-439-07969-1.

■ **PICTURE BOOK**
■ **AGES 5–9**

Summary

Eleven award-winning illustrators provide the rich, colorful illustrations that augment the poetic text celebrating the wonders of creation. An alphabetical glossary at the end of the book identifies the illustrators, types of illustrations, words related to the verses and illustrations, and definitions of the words. Recurring text throughout the book is "the blue and green Ark adrift in the dark."

Bookwalk

Introduce the book by showing the illustrations and reading aloud the accompanying verses. Invite the group to chime in on the recurring line "the blue and green Ark adrift in the dark." To read aloud the entire book may take more time than you want to spend, but you can show illustrations and read aloud selected pages to encourage children to select and read the entire book.

Curriculum Connections

Develop oral language by encouraging children to select and read aloud their favorite verses. Introduce and develop the art of "performing" poetry. Continue with other books by Brian Patten and with books by Ashley Bryan.

Use this book as a model for using the alphabet to write verse or lyrical text. Encourage students to write and illustrate their own group alphabet book celebrating creation.

Related Books

Other collections of verse by Brian Patten are *Gargling with Jelly* and *Thawing Frozen Frogs*. Use his books in conjunction with a study of poetry, particularly poetry readings and the performance of poetry.

Rose, Deborah Lee. **Into the A, B, Sea**. New York: Scholastic Press, 2000. Unpaged. $15.95. ISBN 0-439-09696-0.

■ **PICTURE BOOK—ESOL**
■ **AGES 3–8**

Summary

Cut-paper collages, the colors of marine life and the marine world, provide the background for the simple three- and four-word rhyming lines that describe the sea life featured in this alphabet book. The book ends with an alphabetical list of more information about the featured sea life.

Read-Aloud

Introduce this colorful alphabet book by showing the illustrations to the children and reading aloud the simple lines that name and describe the featured sea life.

Curriculum Connections

Have the children write their own alphabet books using three- and four-word rhyming lines. Encourage them to illustrate their books with cut-paper collages. You can also use this book to launch the study of cut-paper collage as an art form or in conjunction with a study of marine life. The clarity of the illustrations and simplicity of the text make it appropriate for use with English speakers of other languages (ESOL).

Related Books

Other illustrators of children's picture books who use cut-paper collage are Lois Ehlert and Denise Fleming.

FANTASY AND ADVENTURE

Coville, Bruce. **Song of the Wanderer**. New York: Scholastic Press, 1999. 338p. $16.95. ISBN 0-590-45953-8.

■ **CHAPTER BOOK**
■ **AGES 8–12**

Summary

In this second book of the Unicorn Chronicles Series, Cara undertakes a perilous journey through the land of Luster in order to return to Earth to save her grandmother.

Booktalk

Dragons, goblin-like creatures, spells, and unicorns accompany Cara, a human child, on her perilous journey through the land of Luster. Cara holds the amulet that her grandmother gave her to make the leap from Luster to Earth. But the crossing must be made from exactly the right place and only the geomancer can help Cara to determine exactly the right place for the crossing. What are the most dangerous parts of Cara's journey? Why the spells and trickery of Beloved, Cara's own ancestor, who hates the unicorns and is determined to destroy them?

Curriculum Connections

After students have read the book, have them identify and discuss the creatures and characters. Develop a character wheel of Cara, her grandmother, Beloved, Arabella Skydancer, or Moonheart (see Appendix A). Retell the story by retracing the path and events of Cara's journey. Use a fish bone (see Appendix A) to record the retelling. Extend the book to include art and drama by having students create puppets or papier-mâché figures of their favorite characters (e.g., dragons, goblin-like creatures, unicorns, Cara, Cara's grandmother, Arabella Skydancer, or Moonheart), or make maps of the lands of Luster and Summerhaven. You may want to use the salt dough recipe in Appendix B to create relief maps that students can paint and embellish. Encourage students to act out episodes from the book using their puppets, papier-mâché figures, and maps.

Related Books

Other books about unicorns by Bruce Coville are listed on the inside back cover of *Song of the Wanderer*. *Nobody Rides a Unicorn* by Adrian Mitchell and *The Magic of Mythical Creatures* by Colleayn O. Mastin are picture books that are reviewed in this section.

Ernest, Lisa Campbell. **Goldilocks Returns**. New York: Simon & Schuster, 2000. Unpaged. $16.00. ISBN 0-689-82537-4.

■ **PICTURE BOOK**
■ **AGES 4–8**

Summary

Fifty years after the three bears incident, Goldilocks has grown up and returns to their cottage to make amends for the damage she caused when she was a little girl.

Booktalk

Do you remember the story of Goldilocks and the three bears? Well, even after she grew up, Goldilocks never forgot what a naughty little girl she had been to cause so much damage in the three bears' little cottage. One day Goldi (that's what people call her now) closed her locksmith shop and drove off into the woods to the three bears' cottage. The bears had gone off for a walk while their porridge cooled on the kitchen table so now was her chance to make amends. What do you think Goldi did? And what do you suppose Mama, Papa, and Baby Bear said when they returned home?

Curriculum Connections

Although the book is recommended for ages 4–8, older students are likely to enjoy the humor of this story. Read other stories based on familiar nursery and fairy tales. Have children write their own continuations of familiar tales. For example, what happened to Snow White after she married the prince? What kind of job did Little Red Riding Hood get when she grew up?

Related Books

A Wolf at the Door and Other Retold Fairy Tales edited by Ellen Datlow and Terri Windling is a collection of thirteen stories based on familiar fairy tales. It is reviewed in the section Short Stories, Humor, Riddles, and Puzzles.

Kirk, David. **Nova's Ark**. New York: Scholastic Press, 1999. 40p. $17.95. ISBN 0-590-28208-5.

■ **PICTURE BOOK**
■ **AGES 5–8**

Summary

From the author of the Miss Spider books comes a science fiction fantasy—the space adventure of a young robot in search of the universe's source of power. A little bit of Superman sprinkled with Geppeto, mixed well with the television series *Star Trek* and the Old Testament account of Noah and his ark, seasoned liberally with imagination and creativity serve up a brand new story. Bold, brilliant, full-page illustrations using 3-D computer imaging augment the text.

Booktalk

Nova's teacher often told him, "Someday you'll fly into space like your father." That day came when Nova, a young robot, visited the Space Center with his classmates. While waiting with his classmates for a hover bus to take them home from the Space Center, Nova wandered back to the Glax Cruiser for one more look. When he pulled the lever that activated the ship, his teacher's words came true. The ship took off. Now what? Where will Nova end up? Will he run out of fuel?

Curriculum Connections

Invite students to retell the story and imagine that they are helping the author develop a motion picture script that features Nova as the star. Have students create a storyboard that blocks the scenes and action of the story. Some students might want to retell the story by using Lego™ pieces to build Nova, his menagerie, Nova's father, and their spaceships.

Lester, Julius, and Joe Cepeda. **What a Truly Cool World**. New York: Scholastic Press, 1999. Unpaged. $15.95. ISBN 0-590-86468-8.

■ **PICTURE BOOK—Fantasy; African Americans**
■ **ALL AGES**

Summary

In this fractured creation story, God is rather pleased with himself after he creates the world, but his angel Shaniqua says that it all looks boring. With a lot of help from Shaniqua and her angel friends, God transforms the boring world into a really cool world.

Booktalk

"What you call that down there?" Shaniqua, the angel in charge of everybody's business, tells God that the world he has just created looks kind of boring. God looks again at his world and sees that Shaniqua is right. But he doesn't quite know what to do. He calls for Bruce his secretary, has coffee with his wife Irene God, and asks for help from Shaniqua. And that was only the beginning of the "truly cool world"!

Curriculum Connections

This is a book to be read aloud for the humorous dialogue between God and his angels. Encourage children to retell the story by selecting roles, writing, practicing, and presenting a readers' theater version. You will need a narrator, God, the angels Shaniqua and Bruce, somebody, and choral reading of musical flower names, the flowers, flutterby tears, and people.

Mastin, Colleayn O. **The Magic of Mythical Creatures**. Kamloops, BC: Grasshopper Books, 1997. 32p. Illustrated by Jan Sovak. $17.95. ISBN 1-895910-45-5.

■ **PICTURE BOOK**
■ **AGES 7–14**

Summary

Fifteen mythical creatures are introduced to the reader using a two-page spread. Full-color illustrations on the right-hand pages are accompanied by informative text on the left-hand pages.

Booktalk/Bookwalk

(Show the pictures as you talk about the creatures.) Have you ever wondered about dragons of fire, mermaids, trolls, unicorns, or other creatures? Dragons of fire are evil and mean (page 6). Mermaids can swim from one ocean to the next and have beautiful faces and lovely singing voices (page 12). Trolls are ugly creatures who steal from humans (page 20). But maybe they'll be nice if you give them a plate of bananas and cream. Unicorns look like white horses, with lions' tails, and horns in the middle of their foreheads (page 28). Fairy princesses like to ride them in the woods. They sleep with their eyes open and can see with their eyes shut. Which is your favorite? What else can you learn about these mythical creatures?

Curriculum Connections

Ask children which of the mythical creatures in the book they have heard about and what they know about the creatures. Gather and set up a display of poetry and books in which mythical creatures appear and have each child choose a poem or book, for example, Hans Christian Andersen's *The Little Mermaid* or *The Three Billy Goats Gruff* (with its mythical troll). Then talk about the poetry and books and their mythical creatures.

Nikly, Michelle. **The Perfume of Memory**. New York: Arthur A. Levine Books, 1998. Unpaged. $16.95. ISBN 0-439-08206-4.

■ **PICTURE BOOK—North Africa**
■ **AGES 7–10**

Summary

Yasmin, a perfume-maker's daughter, restores the Queen's memory after the evil Royal Advisor creates a perfume that causes the Queen to forget who she is.

Booktalk

Once upon a time, in a far and distant land, only boys could become perfume-makers. In that far and distant land, the people began to forget things such as their history, each other's birthdays, the endings of songs, and how to think for themselves. They even forgot that once upon a time even girls were allowed to become perfume-makers.

Yasmin, the perfume-maker's daughter, watches everything her father does and even makes perfumes of her own. One day she gathers all of the scents that remind her of her mother (who died when she was born), her father, and herself.

Curriculum Connections

Have children use the text to write a script. Using the illustrations and descriptions as a guide, have children make puppets (plastic spoons with painted faces, yarn hair glued onto the spoon, and scraps of fabric for clothing). Finally, have them retell the story by putting on a puppet show for other children.

Pilkey, Dav. **Ricky Ricotta's Giant Robot**. New York: Blue Sky Press, 2000. 111p. Illustrated by Martin Ontiveros. $16.95. ISBN 0-590-30719-3.

■ **CHAPTER BOOK**
■ **AGES 6–10**

Summary

Reluctant and not-so-reluctant readers will equally enjoy the cartoon-like illustrations and limited text that tell this story. A little mouse and his giant flying robot do battle with the evil Dr. Stinky. Flip the pages and watch the illustrations move. Instructions for drawing the Robot and the Monster are included in the back of the book.

Booktalk/Bookwalk

Have you ever had a robot? Have you ever had a robot for a friend? Well Ricky did. Meet Ricky and his Robot. (Flip the Robot pages 25–35.) Ricky and the Robot weren't always friends. But Ricky was watching when the Robot refused to destroy Squeakyville and the evil Dr. Stinky zapped him with a shock from the remote control. Ricky saved the Robot by kicking a kickball into the back of Dr. Stinky's head. That was the day the Robot followed Ricky home from school. Then the trouble with Dr. Stinky really began!

Curriculum Connections

Encourage the children to write and illustrate their own stories about Ricky and the Robot. Follow the directions in the back of the book. Have the children draw cartoons of the Robot and the Monster and create flip pages like those in the book.

Related Books

Other books about Ricky Ricotta and his Giant Robot are *Ricky Ricotta's Giant Robot vs. The Mutant Mosquitoes from Mercury* and *Ricky Ricotta's Giant Robot vs. The Voodoo Vultures from Venus*. An entire series of books is planned.

The Captain Underpants Series is another series of flip books by Dav Pilkey. They tell stories about Captain Underpants who does battle with the talking toilets, the incredibly naughty cafeteria ladies from outer space, and Professor Poopypants.

Pullman, Philip. **The Fire-Maker's Daughter.** New York: Arthur A. Levine Books, 1999. 97p. $15.95. ISBN 0-590-18719-8.

■ **CHAPTER BOOK—India**
■ **AGES 8–12**

Summary

Lila, a fireworks-maker's daughter, wants to become a fireworks-maker just like her father. Her father, however, wants her to marry. In order to become a fireworks-maker, Lila must be tested for the Three Gifts and then make a long journey to the Grotto of Razvani the Fire-Fiend to get some of the royal sulphur. The text is interspersed with humor and wordplay.

Booktalk

Do you know what you want to be when you grow up? Well, Lila knows what she wants to do when she grows up. She wants to become a fireworks-maker just like her father. Unfortunately, her father wants her to marry. Now she needs to make the long journey to the Grotto of Razvani the Fire-Fiend to get some of the royal sulphur. She packs a few belongings, leaves a note for her father, and sets off for the Grotto. What Lila doesn't know is that to make this long journey she needs the protection of magic water from the Goddess of the Emerald Lake. And so Lila's adventure begins.

Curriculum Connections

Use a Venn diagram to compare and contrast this book with *The Perfume of Memory* by Michelle Nikly. Both stories are about two girls whose mothers have died. The girls learn their fathers' trades, one a perfume-maker, the other a fireworks-maker. Both girls want to follow in their fathers' footsteps but are forbidden to do so. One girl enters a contest; the other must be tested for the Three Gifts and then makes a long journey.

Rowling, J. K. **Harry Potter and the Sorcerer's Stone**. New York: Arthur A. Levine Books (an imprint of Scholastic Press), 2000. 734p. Illustrated by Mary Grandpré. $25.95. ISBN 0-439-13959-7.

- **CHAPTER BOOK**
- **AGES 8 and up**

Summary

Harry Potter, a young wizard, is a student at Hogwart's School of Witchcraft and Wizardry where the forces of good and evil engage in battle. Humor, adventure, magic, mystery, and fantasy characterize this controversial series that is being read by children and adults of all ages around the English-speaking world. It has also been made into a movie.

Booktalk

Harry didn't know anything about being a wizard, at least not until the letters started coming. Then Hagrid showed up on Harry's birthday and told Harry that he had been accepted at Hogwart's School of Witchcraft and Wizardry. When Harry goes off to school, he knows it's going to be an interesting year.

Curriculum Connections

The size of the book lends itself to selecting a chapter to read aloud and engaging students in sampling, predicting, and confirming what might happen next. Have children who have seen the movie compare the book with the movie. Students might also enjoy retelling through puppetry, model building, mask making, and acting out activities based on these books. As students read, have them block the scenes and action of the story to create a roll movie. Select or compose music and use rhythm instruments as background for the roll movie.

Related Books

Other books in the Harry Potter Series are *Harry Potter and the Chamber of Secrets, Harry Potter and the Prisoner of Azkaban,* and *Harry Potter and the Goblet of Fire.*

MYSTERIES

Byars, Betsy. **Disappearing Acts.** New York: Viking, 1998. 120p. $14.99. ISBN 0-670-87735-2.

- ■ **CHAPTER BOOK**
- ■ **AGES 9–12**

Summary

It is bad enough that the dead girl's body disappears. Then Herculeah picks up her pictures and starts acting peculiar. Meat has two mysteries to solve.

Booktalk

First a dead girl's body disappears. Then Herculeah picks up her pictures and starts acting very peculiar. After that, Meat leaves and doesn't come back. Now Herculeah is searching for Meat. She enters a building, but hears voices and ducks into the janitor's closet. The voices approach, talking about the dead body. Suddenly Herculeah realizes those voices are about to find her. She feels a scream rising within her when suddenly a hand clasps around her mouth.

Curriculum Connections

The suspenseful ending of each chapter lends itself to asking listeners or readers to listen or read, predict what will happen next, then listen or read to confirm their predictions.

Related Books

Other books in the Herculeah Jones Series are *Dead Letter*, *Death's Door*, *Tarot Says Beware*, and *The Dark Stairs*.

Shreve, Susan. **Ghost Cats**. New York: Arthur A. Levine Books, 1999. 128p. $14.95. ISBN 0-590-37131-2.

■ **CHAPTER BOOK—Families**
■ **AGES 8–12**

Summary

When Peter and his family settle in Boston permanently after years of moving from one country to another, Peter's life changes in ways he doesn't like. His sisters make new friends, his brother is diagnosed with a learning disability, and his mother goes back to school. Then the family's lost cats reappear!

Booktalk

Peter's life was always changing. Every year or so he and his family moved from one country to another—and he loved it. Now the family has settled in Boston—permanently. Peter does not love the changes that are happening. His sisters are making new friends and are not interested in hanging out with him. His brother is diagnosed with a learning disability and spends more and more time with a tutor. Even his mother isn't around much anymore. She's decided to go back to school. Suddenly the family's cats that had died or disappeared begin to show up again! Are they real or are they ghosts?

Curriculum Connections

Ask the children, "Were the cats real or were they ghosts? What do you think and why?" This would also be a good book to use for a discussion of change in our lives. Ask students what kinds of changes they have experienced in their lives and how they learned to live with those changes.

Related Books

Other books that address the topic of change are included in Chapter 3, "Social Studies," in the section "Relationships and Coming of Age."

Wilson, Eric. **Murder on the Canadian**. Custer, WA: Orca, 2000. 144p. $4.99. ISBN 1-55143-172-6.

■ **CHAPTER BOOK**
■ **AGES 9–12**

Summary

In this Eric Wilson Mystery starring Tom Austen, the beautiful Catherine Saks is murdered in her bedroom aboard *The Canadian* as the train travels across Canada from Winnipeg to Vancouver. Catherine's husband, Richard, is immediately arrested. Young Tom Austen isn't convinced that Richard is the murderer and decides to do some investigating of his own.

Booktalk

First there was one shriek, then another. Tom pulled on his jeans and climbed out of his berth. When he ran into the bedroom corridor of the train he saw Richard Saks holding a bloody knife. Richard's beautiful wife, Catherine, was dead, stabbed again and again. Now all of the evidence points to Richard Saks. But Tom isn't convinced that he is the murderer, and he decides to do some investigating of his own.

Curriculum Connections

Catherine Saks is murdered at the end of Chapter 5. Her husband is arrested at the end of Chapter 6. Have students discuss why Tom is not convinced that Richard Saks is the murderer. Identify other suspects. Silently read Chapter 7. Discuss suspects and clues. Predict who the murderer might be. Then silently read Chapter 8 in which the murderer is revealed.

Related Books

Other books in the Eric Wilson Mystery Series are: *Disneyland Hostage*, *Vancouver Nightmare*, and *Code Red at the Supermall*. Opening chapters of all of the Eric Wilson Mysteries are available for reading at the author's Web site: http://www.ericwilson.com.

Wright, Betty Ren. **The Moonlight Man**. New York: Scholastic Press, 2000. 176p. $15.95. ISBN 0-590-25237-2.

- ■ **CHAPTER BOOK**
- ■ **AGES 8–12**

Summary

Fifteen-year-old Jenny and her six-year-old sister, Allie, think they have found home, at last, when they move into the little house in the woods.

Booktalk

From the beginning something was peculiar. First, there was the picture in Allie's room that disappeared and reappeared. Then there was the man with the dog who appeared in the moonlight and disappeared. And what was the crying in April's basement? The Carpeks were peculiar too. Jenny knew that she couldn't talk to her dad. He'd want to move again. So would April's parents, if the girls went to them. Jenny and April would just have to solve this mystery by themselves.

Curriculum Connections

Have children list clues to the unfolding mystery as they read. Discuss the clues and predict what they might mean. Then read to confirm predictions. Create a chart listing the clues, predictions, and confirmations.

Related Books

Award-winning books by Betty Ren Wright are *Christina's Ghost*, *Ghosts Beneath Our Feet*, and *The Dollhouse Murders*. Other titles are listed in the back of this book.

POETRY

Adoff, Arnold, and Lisa Desimini. **Touch the Poem**. New York: Blue Sky Press, 2000. Unpaged. $16.95. ISBN 0-590-47970-9.

■ **PICTURE BOOK**
■ **AGES 7–12**

Summary

Poems that celebrate the senses practically dance off the pages. Mixed-media collages illustrate the lively text.

Booktalk/Bookwalk/Read-Aloud

(As you page through the book, ask the children to respond to these questions.) What do you like to taste? Smell? Feel? Touch? French pastries for breakfast? A rainy spring morning? Relaxing on the beach? Soaking in the tub? Finger painting? Here's a poem about _____. (Select a poem to read aloud.)

Curriculum Connections

Many of these poems lend themselves to recitation and acting out through creative dramatics. Have students select a poem to read or recite to the class. Select or compose background music. You might also have students list their own sensory experiences, then write poems about them.

Gershator, Phyllis, and David Gershator. **Greetings Sun**. New York: DK, 1998. Unpaged. Illustrated by Synthia Saint James. ISBN 0-7894-2482-7.

■ **PICTURE BOOK—Verse**
■ **ALL AGES**

Summary

Two young children, a boy and a girl, greet the day from morning through night with a simple rhyming text. According to the book jacket, African praise songs were the inspiration for this book. The rhythm of the repetitive "Greeting . . ." is similar to the rhythmic repetitive text of *Goodnight Moon* by Margaret Wise Brown, and the bold, colorful, simple collage-type illustrations are similar to the montage illustrations of *A Snowy Day* by Ezra Jack Keats.

Read-Aloud

Read aloud and show the pictures.

Curriculum Connections

Have children greet the day and write their greetings using a simple rhyme. Some may want to illustrate their greetings with boldly colored construction paper collages.

Kirk, David. **Little Miss Spider: Sunny Patch School.** New York: Scholastic Press, 2000. Unpaged. $12.95. ISBN 0-439-08727-9.

■ **PICTURE BOOK—Verse**
■ **AGES 3–7**

Summary

Four-line verses and brilliant oil paintings tell the story of Little Miss Spider at school where she discovered that her special gift was the gift of kindness. This is a warm, cozy book to read and enjoy.

Booktalk

Little Miss Spider dreamed of going to school, and of all the wonderful things she would learn—to climb, to cling, to know about flowers, and to tunnel through fruit. But Little Miss Spider had no talent. She wasn't very strong, and she was useless at stinging. Little Miss Spider was so unhappy. Then she found a little bug that was stuck in a spout. That was when she discovered that she had the greatest gift of all.

Curriculum Connections

Show the pictures and read aloud before nap time or dismissal. Make the book available in the classroom library corner for voluntary reading. Use with other Miss Spider books. Encourage the children to orally tell or write their own stories about Miss Spider. Invite the children to retell the story and imagine that they are helping the author write a movie screenplay about Miss Spider. Encourage the children to create roll movies about her. Extend the book into a science lesson by having the children learn more about spiders and asking them to draw a picture of what they have learned. Create a spider farm.

Related Books

Other books about Miss Spider are *Miss Spider's ABC*, *Miss Spider's New Car*, *Miss Spider's Wedding*, *Miss Spider's Tea Party*, and *Miss Spider's Tea Party: The Counting Book*.

Miller, Joe. **If the Earth . . . Were a Few Feet in Diameter.** Shelton, CT: Greenwich Workshop Press, 1998. Unpaged. Illustrated by Wilson McLean. $16.95. ISBN 0-86713-054-7.

■ **PICTURE BOOK—Verse**
■ **ALL AGES**

Summary

With one line per two-page spread, nine lines of poetic text augmented by full-page colored illustrations invite the reader to wonder, cherish, and love Earth. Mathematical facts are presented in four sidebars. The last page is a retelling with the nine lines written in the shape of a sphere.

Read-Aloud

This is a book to be seen and heard. Read aloud and show the pictures.

Curriculum Connections

Use as a model to celebrate Earth. Talk about the things the children love, cherish, and wonder about. Have each child write and illustrate one line. Then compile children's illustrations with one-line captions into a group book that celebrates Earth.

Nye, Naomi Shihab. **Come with Me: Poems for a Journey.** New York: Greenwillow Books, 2000. 32p. Illustrated by Dan Yaccarino. $15.95. ISBN 0-688-15946-X.

■ **PICTURE BOOK**
■ **AGES 7 and up**

Summary

Mixed-media collages illustrate the sixteen poems, which invite the reader to enter a variety of journeys. One journey invitation says "come," another says "watch," and yet another asks "where?" Others are about the map, the envelope, and the return of spring.

Booktalk

All aboard! We're going for a ride on the poetry train. Poems can take you anywhere. Who knows what you'll see or where you'll go? You can spin, share secrets, and even meet Pete. You'll stop at the corner, listen to somebody's story, and maybe find a map. You can board an airplane, and even fly to the moon. Listen. (Read a lively excerpt such as "Torn Map.")

Curriculum Connections

Select poems to read aloud for the joy of experiencing the sounds of language (e.g., repetitive phrases such as "in time, in time," rhythms such as "something shines but nothing moves," and similes such as "with a sleep as deep as desert sand"). Follow up by having students write travel poems and create shape books using trains, buses, automobiles, airplanes, or boats. Have fun with hot-air balloon or scooter journeys. Extend the book by having students use rhythm instruments as accompaniment or have them select or compose background music.

Rash, Andy. **The Robots Are Coming.** New York: Arthur A. Levine Books, 2000. Unpaged. $15.95. ISBN 0-439-06306-X.

■ **PICTURE BOOK—Verse**
■ **AGES 7–12**

Summary

Scary comic-book-like cartoons illustrate sixteen scary poems about robots, voodoo, clones and androids, pirates, giant ants, a mummy, a werewolf, the Loch Ness Monster, and other scary things.

Read-Aloud

Select poems such as "The Robots Are Coming" and "Pirate" to read aloud. Use a dramatic, expressive voice.

Curriculum Connections

Create a scary atmosphere by turning off the lights and using a green-shaded banker's lamp for lighting. Encourage children to select their favorite poems and read them aloud, using gestures and facial expressions as well as their voices to dramatize the poems.

Schneider, Christine M. **Picky Mrs. Pickle**. New York: Walker, 1999. 32p. $15.95. ISBN 0-8027-8702-9.

■ **PICTURE BOOK—Verse**
■ **AGES 5–8**

Summary

Deep colors, bold illustrations, and the simple text written in verse introduce picky Mrs. Pickle who wants her life to be exactly the way she wants it until her youngest niece, stubborn Sophie, speaks her mind.

Booktalk

Have you ever known a picky person? Picky Mrs. Pickle liked her life exactly the way it was, with green dresses and shoes in her closet, with pickle pie and pickle perfume, and the same old hairdo, hat, and friends. Every Sunday afternoon Mrs. Pickle took a walk with her youngest niece, stubborn Sophie. Every week they argued because Mrs. Pickle wouldn't try a new flavor of ice cream. Then Sophie figured out a way to talk her aunt into trying something new. Mrs. Pickle ordered eggplant ripple ice cream and suddenly her life began to change!

Curriculum Connections

Divide children into groups of three. Assign roles: Narrator, Mrs. Pickle, Sophie. Have children read, practice, and reread the book using a readers' theater approach.

Scruggs, Afi. **Jump Rope Magic**. New York: Blue Sky Press, 2000. Unpaged. Illustrated by David Diaz. $16.95. ISBN 0-590-69327-1.

◼ **PICTURE BOOK—Verse; Music; Movement**
◼ **AGES 5–8**

Summary

Vibrant illustrations augment an equally vibrant text that bounces and sings with the rhythm and the music of jump rope rhymes, and the story of Shameka and her jump rope friends.

Booktalk/Read-Aloud

"Our hands are high, our feet are low, and this is the way that we jig-a-low." Shameka and her friends jump rope, and Shameka sings rhymes. "Cinderella dressed in yellow went upstairs to meet her fellow." Then mean Miss Minnie got mad, but Shameka had a song for that too. So what do you suppose Miss Minnie did? (Read aloud and invite children to chime in with the rhymes and the rhythms of this book such as "jig-a-low, jig-a-low," "and-uh-one, and-uh-two," or "shimmy, shimmy bop.")

Curriculum Connections

Encourage children to create their own jump rope rhymes and to compile them in a book along with familiar jump rope rhymes. Give them starter lines such as "Hannah looked at the great, blue sky," and have students write the rest of the rhyme.

Smith, William Jay. **Around My Room**. New York: Farrar, Straus & Giroux, 2000. 32p. Illustrated by Erik Blegvad. $16.00. ISBN 0-374-30406-8.

■ **PICTURE BOOK**
■ **AGES 5–10**

Summary

This is a collection of twenty-nine poems including limericks and even a jump rope rhyme. It will delight young children with humor, rhyme, rhythm, and wordplay.

Booktalk/Read-Aloud

Introduce the book by reading aloud short poems such as "The Mirror," "Having," or "The Toaster" on pages 8–9 or a limerick such as "There Was a Young Lady Named Rose" on page 22. Have children repeat lines or words.

Curriculum Connections

Encourage children to select, practice, and read aloud their favorite poems from this collection. Introduce other collections of children's poetry and have children compile a class collection of their favorites.

RETELLINGS

Aylesworth, Jim. **Aunt Pitty Patty's Piggy.** New York: Scholastic Press, 1999. Unpaged. Illustrated by Barbara McClintock. $15.95. ISBN 0-590-89967-2.

■ **PICTURE BOOK—Cumulative tale**
■ **AGES 3–7**

Summary

This is a retelling of the cumulative tale in which Aunt Pitty Patty buys a piggy that will not go through the garden gate. On the back cover of the book is a recipe for Aunt Pitty Patty's corn bread.

Booktalk

Aunt Pitty Patty cannot get her pig through the garden gate. Her niece, Little Nellie, wants to help but cannot do it alone. Who else will lend a hand? The dog? The stick? The fire? Who will help Little Nellie, and how will she solve the problem?

Curriculum Connections

Read aloud showing the pictures on each page. Invite children to chime in on the repetition of "No, no, no, I will not go!" and to retell the story using a flannel board. Bake and serve Aunt Pitty Patty's corn bread. The recipe is in the book.

Daly, Jude. **Fair, Brown, and Trembling: An Irish Cinderella Story.** New York: Farrar, Straus & Giroux, 2000. Unpaged. $16.00. ISBN 0-374-32247-3.

■ **PICTURE BOOK—Irish**
■ **AGES 7–10**

Summary

Trembling is the beautiful sister left at home while her sisters, Fair and Brown, go to church on Sunday. The hen-wife gives Trembling beautiful dresses to wear and horses to ride to church. Now Prince Emania wants to marry her. Once he finds her, he has to fight other princes for her. They marry, have fourteen children, and put the wicked sisters to sea in a barrel with provisions to last for seven years.

Booktalk

You know the story of Cinderella, but do you know the story of Trembling? Trembling was a beautiful Irish girl whose sisters were afraid that she would marry before they did. Every Sunday her sisters left Trembling at home while they went to church wearing lovely new clothes. The hen-wife brought Trembling beautiful dresses to wear with matching horses to ride to church. Prince Emania wanted to marry the strange and beautiful woman, but so did other princes. Who do you suppose would marry Trembling? What would happen to her sisters?

Curriculum Connections

Use a Venn diagram to compare and contrast two variations of the Cinderella story. Have children read the three Cinderella stories reviewed in this section. Have them write a scenario in which Trembling meets Cinderella the Dog and Little Gold Star and the three Cinderellas get acquainted and share their stories.

Related Books

Cinderella the Dog and Her Little Glass Slipper by Diane Goode and *Little Gold Star: A Spanish American Cinderella Tale* by Robert San Souci are other variations of the Cinderella story that are reviewed in this section.

Demi. **The Emperor's New Clothes**. New York: Margaret K. McElderry, 2000. Unpaged. $19.95. ISBN 0-689-83068-8.

■ **PICTURE BOOK—China**
■ **AGES 3 and up**

Summary

Demi's retelling, set in ancient provincial China, unfolds across four seasons and is elegantly illustrated with authentic representations of Chinese culture. Lavish use of gold leaf, foldout pages, and brilliant details make this book a work of art.

Booktalk

The Emperor of China loved new clothes. Everyday he put on new clothes and walked about so his people could admire him. He had spinners, weavers, and tailors who worked day and night throughout the year making fine garments for him to wear. One day a man and a woman came to his palace and offered him the finest clothes in all the world—clothes made with magic so that only clever people could see them. Fools could not. Of course, the Emperor wanted the magical clothes that fools could not see. As the man and the woman wove the cloth, then cut and sewed the clothes, neither the Prime Minister nor the High Chancellor could see anything but an empty loom and empty table. What were they to do? When the man and the woman brought the magical clothes to the Emperor, he didn't want to admit that he could see nothing. Then the Emperor walked through the village so his people could admire him. What do you suppose the people saw?

Curriculum Connections

With older students identify the symbolism that is found on every page, represented in the screen on pages 9–10, and explained in the "Author's Note" in the back of the book. Discuss the contrast between the symbols of purity and virtue found throughout the book and the Emperor's vanity, the courtiers' deception, and the tailors' trickery. Extend the book by using it in conjunction with a unit on China. Use this book, in particular the foldout pages, to introduce students to Chinese art forms such as folios and screens that depict the unfolding of a story and a journey. Read aloud using Chinese music in the background. ("Qu Wenzhong jie qing jiao siang su miao Wut Man Chung festival sketches" is orchestral music of Chinese folk songs, Accession Number OCLC: 46915417.)

Related Books

The Dinosaur's New Clothes by Diane Goode is also reviewed in this section.

Diakite, Baba Waque. **The Hatseller and the Monkeys**. New York: Scholastic Press, 1999. Unpaged. $15.95. ISBN 0-590-96069-5.

■ **PICTURE BOOK—West Africa**
■ **AGES 5–8**

Summary

This variation of the folktale about the hatseller and the monkeys that you might recognize as the story *Caps for Sale* (see "Related Books" below) is a retelling of a West African folktale. The hatseller who loses his hats to the monkeys must figure out a way to get them back.

Booktalk

(You can pantomime BaMusa's actions as you tell this story.) BaMusa the hatmaker set out to sell his hats, which were stacked one atop the other on his head. He left home early in the morning with no breakfast and became very tired and hungry on his way to the village. He sat down under a tree for a nap, stacking his hats beside him. When he awoke, his hats were gone. The monkeys had taken them and now BaMusa must get them back. BaMusa called for help. What do you think happened?

Curriculum Connections

The author retells this authentic West African teaching tale as it was told to him as a child in his small village in Mali, West Africa. The "Author's Note" in the back of the book elaborates on the cultural background of this tale that has been retold in Egypt, Sudan, and India as well as many other countries. This book is illustrated with vibrant, ceramic-tile paintings bordered by a black-and-white monkey motif that was popular in European art during and after the Middle Ages. Sounds of BaMusa's song, his snoring, and the chattering of the monkeys add the dimension of sound effects to the story.

Read then compare and contrast variations of this story using sources listed in the "Author's Note" in the back of the book. Invite children to orally retell the story. Some may want to act out the story with sound effects and an assortment of caps for props. The authenticity of the retelling and illustrations make this book an appropriate selection to celebrate Black History Month.

Related Books

The "Author's Note" at the end of the book cites the following books that include variations of the story: Bulatkin, I. F. *Eurasian Folk and Fairy Tales.* New York: Criterion, 1965; Carpenter, Frances. *African Wonder Tales.* Garden City, NY: Doubleday, 1963; Slobodkina, Esphyr. *Caps for Sale.* Reading, MA: Addison-Wesley, 1940; William-Ellis, Amabel. *Fairy Tales from the British Isles.* New York: Warne, 1960, 1964.

Goode, Diane. **The Dinosaur's New Clothes.** New York: Blue Sky Press, 1999. Unpaged. $15.95. ISBN 0-590-38360-4.

■ **PICTURE BOOK—France**
■ **AGES 3 and up**

Summary

This retelling of Hans Christian Andersen's "The Emperor's New Clothes" is set at the Palace of Versailles during the late eighteenth century when fashions were elaborate and ornate. Dinosaurs such as Tyrannosaurus Rex, Iguanodon, and Stegosaurus people the story and are dressed in powdered wigs and period costumes. The setting, period, and dinosaurs are authentically represented in the illustrations. The two-page spread that introduces the book shows a panoramic view of the Palace of Versailles, its grounds, and the surrounding countryside.

Booktalk/Bookwalk

(Turn pages of the book to show children the illustrations as you talk.) Once there was a kingdom of great dinosaurs. But the Emperor of the Dinosaurs was vain. He spent all of his money on clothes. Every day it was something new, each outfit more lavish than the last. Until, one day when two swindlers came to town.

Curriculum Connections

Extend this book by searching out, collecting, comparing, and contrasting variations on and retellings of familiar folktales and fairy tales. Some examples might be Cinderella, the magic pot, and Foolish Jack tales such as Jack and the Beanstalk. Set up a library or media center display of titles that you have in your collection. Include nonprint acquisitions such as audio and videotapes. Using print and nonprint titles in your collection as models, encourage children to write their own variations or retellings. For an immediate response, have students retell the story by acting it out using creative dramatics. Consider leading a media production workshop for teachers and children who want to produce slides, filmstrips, or audio or videotapes of their retellings. Use in social studies with a study of manners, fashions, and style in late-eighteenth-century France or in science with a study of dinosaurs.

Related Books

Cinderella the Dog and Her Little Glass Slipper by Diane Goode is also set in eighteenth-century France with illustrations that authentically represent the time. Another variation of this story is *The Emperor's New Clothes* by Demi that is also reviewed in this section.

Goode, Diane. **Cinderella the Dog and Her Little Glass Slipper.**
New York: Blue Sky Press, 2000. Unpaged. $15.95. ISBN 0-439-
07166-6.

- **PICTURE BOOK—France**
- **AGES 3 and up**

Summary

This variation of the Cinderella story is set in eighteenth-century
France with different breeds of dogs dressed in period costumes.

Booktalk/Bookwalk

(Show the pictures as you retell the story.) Once upon a time, a
sweet and kind daughter was treated like a servant by her wicked step-
mother and stepsisters. Because she sat among the cinders and the
ashes in the chimney corner, she was called Cinderella (pages 1–2).
One day the stepsisters were invited to a ball given by the king's son
(pages 5–6). After the stepsisters left for the party, a fairy godmother
appeared and asked Cinderella if she would like to go to the party too.
Of course, Cinderella said yes (pages 7–8). The fairy godmother
turned a pumpkin into a coach, mice into horses, and a rat into a foot-
man (pages 9–10). She even turned Cinderella's tattered clothes into a
beautiful gown and glass slippers (pages 11–12). Cinderella drove to
the palace (pages 13–14), entered the ballroom (pages 15–16), and par-
tied until the clock struck a quarter to midnight (pages 17–18). She
quickly hurried home before her sisters arrived to tell her about the
beautiful princess whom no one knew (pages 19–20). When Cinderella
went to the second ball, she stayed until midnight and lost her glass
slipper while running from the palace (pages 21–24). Once again she
hurried home before her sisters arrived to tell her about the beautiful
princess who lost her glass slipper (pages 25–26). The prince went in
search of the beautiful princess whose foot would fit the slipper until
he came to the home of Cinderella and her stepsisters (pages 27–28).

Curriculum Connections

Have the children read other variations of the Cinderella story.
Construct and complete a semantic feature analysis chart to compare
and contrast these variations (see Appendix A).

Related Books

The Dinosaur's New Clothes by Diane Goode is also set in eighteenth-century France with the setting, period, and dinosaurs authentically represented in the illustrations.

Other variations of the Cinderella story reviewed in this section are *Fair, Brown, and Trembling: An Irish Cinderella Story* by Jude Daly and *Little Gold Star: A Spanish American Cinderella Tale* by Robert San Souci.

Hamilton, Virginia. **The Girl Who Spun Gold**. New York: Blue Sky Press, 2000. Unpaged. Illustrated by Leo Dillon and Diane Dillon. $16.95. ISBN 0-590-47378-6.

■ **PICTURE BOOK—Multicultural; West Indies**
■ **AGES 5–8**

Summary

This West Indian variant of Rumplestiltskin is fully reviewed in Chapter 4, in the section "Drama."

Johnson, Paul Brett. **Old Dry Frye**. New York: Scholastic Press, 1999. Unpaged. $15.95. ISBN 0-590-37658-6.

■ **PICTURE BOOK**
■ **AGES 5–8**

Summary

This is a retelling of the Appalachian tale of a preacher who loved to eat chicken.

Booktalk

When Old Dry Frye choked on a chicken bone and died at the farmhouse, the farmer and his wife feared that they would be accused of murdering the preacher. The widow, two brothers, and an old man and his wife also believed that they would be accused of murdering the preacher. That night something strange happened. Now why do you suppose folks now say that Old Dry Frye is still riding round the countryside on the old man's horse?

Curriculum Connections

Have children respond by retelling the story using a flannel board.

Olaleye, Isaac O. **In the Rainfield: Who Is the Greatest?** New York: Blue Sky Press, 2000. Unpaged. Illustrated by Ann Grifalconi. $15.95. ISBN 0-590-48363-3.

■ **PICTURE BOOK—Nigeria**
■ **AGES 4–9**

Summary

This retelling of a Nigerian folktale is fully reviewed in Chapter 4, in the section "Drama."

Rosales, Melodye Benson. **Leola and the Honeybears.** New York: Scholastic Press, 1999. 37p. $15.95. ISBN 0-590-38358-2.

■ **PICTURE BOOK—African Americans**
■ **AGES 3–8**

Summary

This is an African American retelling of Goldilocks and the three bears set in the rural South. Deep, rich oil paintings illustrate the text.

Booktalk

Looking back, Leola knew that she should have obeyed when Grandmama said, "Don't go straying off." But Leola said to herself, "I don't care what Grandmama says." She went so far that the next thing she knew she was lost in the woods. Somehow she managed to find her way into the Honeybears' Inn while Papa, Mama, and Baby Honeybear were out fishing for catfish. Inside, there was plum pie, rose petal cobbler, huckleberry tart, and chocolate-covered pine nuts. Leola was so hungry. But now the Honeybear family was on their way home.

Curriculum Connections

Encourage children to retell the story using a flannel board. Select to celebrate Black History Month.

San Souci, Robert D. **Little Gold Star: A Spanish American Cinderella Tale**. New York: HarperCollins, 2000. Unpaged. $15.95. ISBN 0-688-14780-1.

■ **PICTURE BOOK—Spanish Americans; Catholic**
■ **AGES 5 and up**

Summary

This Spanish American variation of Cinderella is set in New Mexico.

Booktalk

Soon after Teresa's father married the widow with two daughters trouble started. It only got worse after the lady dressed in blue placed a gold star on Teresa's forehead. One of the cruel sisters sprouted horns; the other sprouted donkey ears. How do you suppose that happened? Now what in the world is this family to do?

Curriculum Connections

Compare and contrast with other Cinderella stories.

Related Books

Cinderella the Dog and Her Little Glass Slipper by Diane Goode and *Fair, Brown, and Trembling: An Irish Cinderella Story* by Jude Daly are other variations of the Cinderella tale that are reviewed in this section.

Wattenberg, Jane. **Henny-Penny**. New York: Scholastic Press, 2000. Unpaged. $15.95. ISBN 0-439-07817-2.

■ **PICTURE BOOK**
■ **AGES 5–8**

Summary

This "cool" retelling takes Henny-Penny and her friends from Stonehenge to the Sonoran Desert, to the pyramids of Egypt and the Leaning Tower of Pisa, and past the Taj Mahal, the Colosseum of Rome, and the Parthenon of Greece, all on their way to tell the king that the sky is falling.

Bookwalk

Read aloud. Be sure to show the pictures as you retell the story. Invite children to chime in on the repetitive phrase "Shake, rattle, and roll! The sky is falling!" Imagine what Henny-Penny must have thought when an acorn dropped on her head (pages 1–2). Why, she thought the sky was falling (pages 3–4)! As she ran to tell the king, she met Cocky-Locky (pages 5–6), then Ducky-Lucky (pages 7–8) and Goosey-Loosey too (pages 9–10). As they continued on their way, they met Turkey-Lurkey (pages 11–12) and Foxy-Loxy (pages 13–14). Foxy-Loxy offered to lead the way (pages 15–16) as he dreamed about his dinner (pages 17–18). Now, what do you think happened? Did Henny-Penny and her friends tell the king that the sky was falling or did Foxy-Loxy have a fine dinner that night?

Curriculum Connections

Encourage children to join in wordplay that is modeled in the book. Extend the book into a social studies lesson by identifying the landmarks in the illustrations and locating them on a map. With the children, create a map tracing the path of Henny-Penny and her friends.

SHORT STORIES, HUMOR, RIDDLES, AND PUZZLES

Agee, Jon. **Elvis Lives! And Other Anagrams**. New York: Farrar, Straus & Giroux, 2000. Unpaged. $15.00. ISBN 0-374-32127-2.

■ **PICTURE BOOK—Puzzles**
■ **AGES 8–12**

Summary

Humorous cartoons illustrate sixty anagrams such as "Norwegians/ Swen or Inga," "the eyes/they see," and "Eskimoes/some ski."

Booktalk/Bookwalk

Do you know what an anagram is? It's a word or a phrase that is made by rearranging the letters of another word or phrase such as the title of this book. For example, the letters in "Elvis" can be rearranged to make the word "lives." (Randomly show two or three pages with cartoons and anagrams. Then give children two or three anagrams to solve such as "Rodney/yonder," "the loser/lost here," and "life's aim/families.")

Curriculum Connections

Follow up by encouraging children to create their own anagrams. Write and illustrate a class book of anagrams.

Cameron, Ann. **Gloria's Way**. New York: Farrar, Straus & Giroux, 2000. 96p. Illustrated by Lis Toft. $15.00. ISBN 0-374-32670-3.

- **CHAPTER BOOK—Short Stories; African Americans**
- **AGES 7–10**

Summary

Six short, easy-to-read chapters each tell a story about Gloria, an African American girl, and her family and friends.

Booktalk

Maybe you already know Gloria? She is Julian's best friend. Maybe you met her in the stories that you read about Julian and his brother Huey? Huey and Julian have told their stories. Now Gloria has her own stories to tell—about the parrot that wouldn't give back her valentine, about how she cured her dog from chasing squirrels, and others. And, oh yes, Huey and Julian are here in Gloria's stories too.

Curriculum Connections

Use as a model to encourage students to write stories about their daily experiences with families and friends. Have students start keeping a journal. Give them ten to fifteen minutes a day to write in it. Have students create a story map based on one of their journal entries. Identify the setting, characters, problem, solution, and ending and write a story.

Related Books

Additional books by Ann Cameron, including books about Gloria's friends, Julian and Huey, such as *The Stories Huey Tells*, *The Stories Julian Tells*, *Julian's Glorious Summer*, and others, are listed inside the book.

Datlow, Ellen, and Terri Windling, eds. **A Wolf at the Door and Other Retold Fairy Tales**. New York: Simon & Schuster, 2000. 166p. $16.00. ISBN 0-689- 82138-7.

■ **CHAPTER BOOK—Short Stories**
■ **AGES 10–14**

Summary

Thirteen authors such as Jane Yolen, Michael Cadnum, Garth Nix, and others have selected their favorite fairy tales and have each written new versions of them. A short biography of the author and other titles by that author follow each story. Three fairy tale collections and three Web sites are identified following the Introduction.

Booktalk

You've heard the stories about Cinderella, Jack and the Beanstalk, Hansel and Gretel, Snow White, and other familiar fairy tales. Now you can read about Cinder Elephant; Mrs. Big, the wife of Jack's giant; what the dwarfs did after Snow White married her prince; a modern day Hansel and Gretel; and other brand-new stories by your favorite authors. My favorite story is the one about "Ali Baba and the Forty Aliens." Ali's real name was Alberto Babarino. He was named after his uncle. Everyone called his uncle Big Al, so he was Little Al or Ali for short. The kids in school called him Ali Baba.

Ali knew something was wrong before he even met the aliens. Everything looked too neat. The grass was trampled flatter than it should be. The animals and birds were nowhere around and something smelled funny. Then he saw them! Forty of them! Aliens!

Curriculum Connections

Use as a model for writing. Have students select a favorite fairy tale and write a brand-new story by changing names, settings, perspectives, tone, or outcomes.

Related Books

Some students may want to read the fairy tale collections and visit the Web sites listed following the Introduction. Others may want to read additional books by the short-story authors. They may also want to read *Goldilocks Returns* by Lisa Campbell Ernest, which is another new story that's based on a familiar tale and is reviewed in the "Fantasy and Adventure" section.

Fleischman, Sid. **A Carnival of Animals**. New York: Greenwillow Books, 2000. 48p. Illustrated by Marylin Hafner. $15.95. ISBN 0-688-16948-1.

- ■ **CHAPTER BOOK—Humor**
- ■ **AGES 7–12**

Summary

This is a collection of six humorous tall tales about the mischief stirred up by a "no-account little tornado."

Booktalk

One day a "no-account little tornado" blew across the country-side. It kerplunked a Windblown Child who was really a Sidehill Clinger from the mountains right down onto the flatlands. But this was only the beginning. Mad Dog, Yeller Cat, Floyd the rooster, Webster the frog, and the Pitchfork Giant all got in on the action. Find out what happened to J. J. Jones the day a "no-account little tornado" blew in.

Curriculum Connections

Use in conjunction with a unit on tall tales. Have children write additional tall tales about the mischief created by a "no-account little tornado" or another natural disaster.

Marzollo, Jean. **I Spy Extreme Challenger! A Book of Picture Riddles**. New York: Scholastic Press, 2000. 32p. Photographs by Walter Wick. $13.95. ISBN 0-439-19900-X.

■ **PICTURE BOOK—Riddles**
■ **AGES 5 and up**

Summary

Each two-page spread begins with the words "I spy . . ." followed by a list of items to be found in the illustrations. The book ends with two pages of additional rhyming riddles and items to be found in the illustrations and a final page that urges readers to write even more rhyming riddles to be used with the illustrations in the book.

Booktalk/Bookwalk

Select and show a two-page spread, read the rhyming "I spy . . ." riddle, and have children find the items in the illustrations.

Curriculum Connections

Follow up by encouraging children to create their own rhyming riddles to be used with the illustrations in the book. Extend the activity by having the children create their own illustrations and "I spy . . ." riddles. Create illustrations by cutting pictures from magazines and creating a collage.

CHAPTER 2

Mathematics and Science

INTRODUCTION

Pleasure reading isn't often considered a natural complement to mathematics and science, but it should be. The books included in this chapter offer fun, creative, informational, and high-interest recreational reading to young readers—and they can enhance and enliven math and science studies by introducing or reinforcing key concepts and lessons. These concept books, picture books, poetry and rhyming verse collections, and biographies present mathematics and science as the integral parts of life that they really are. There are counting books that can make learning numbers fun. There are books that help teach about shapes, fractions, and time. There are colorful books about the animal and plant worlds. And there are intergenerational books that tell stories of grandparents or elderly adults introducing children to the natural environment. With these titles, exploring the worlds of math and science through books becomes an exciting adventure.

MATHEMATICS

Counting

Anderson, Lena. **Tea for Ten**. New York: Farrar, Straus & Giroux, 2000. Unpaged. Translated by Elizabeth Kallick Dyssegaard. $14.00. ISBN 91-29-64557-3.

■ **PICTURE BOOK—Concept Book**
■ **AGES 3–7**

Summary

Rhyming four-line text and gentle watercolor drawings develop the concept of one to ten when Hedgehog invites her friends for tea.

Booktalk/Bookwalk/Read-Aloud

(Page through the book, showing children the illustrations as you talk.) Lonely little Hedgehog invited her friends to tea. Hedgehog was only one. When Uncle Will came they were two. How many were they when Elephant, Duck, and Teddy came? When frog arrived they were six, and pig made seven. Then came Lotty, monkey, and finally cat. Hedgehog and her friends were how many for tea?

Curriculum Connections

Read aloud and use for repeated readings. Encourage children to chime in by saying the number at the end of each page. Count the number of friends in each picture. Extend the counting to objects in the immediate environment (e.g., the library, media center, or classroom).

Greenstein, Elaine. **Dreaming**. New York: Arthur A. Levine Books, 2000. Unpaged. $15.95. ISBN 0-439-06302-7.

■ **PICTURE BOOK—Concept Book**
■ **AGES 3–7**

Summary

This is a bedtime concept book in which the almost sleeping child dreams of counting backwards from ten houses to one swan. (Note: The child is neither a boy nor a girl, just a child, which supports the text use of the second-person "you.") Numbers are presented numerically and in words with text on one page and the illustration on the facing page. In addition to the items for the current two-page spread, each illustration includes the items that will be featured on the next two-page spread.

Booktalk

How many of you can count from one to ten? Count with me. (Count together from one to ten holding up your fingers to indicate the number.) Do you ever count before going to sleep? This little book (show book) is about a child who counts backwards before going to sleep at night. Can you count backwards? Everyone together, now let's count backwards. (Then count backwards from ten to one. Hold up your fingers to indicate the number.)

Curriculum Connections

Introduce the book with the booktalk, then read aloud and show the pictures. Follow up by counting backwards from ten to one with students. Continue by looking around the room for objects to count, such as five boys, three pieces of chalk, ten books. Rank-order objects from ten to one. Use a chalkboard, white board, or flip chart to record and then rank-order objects. Extend the activity by having each child draw a picture of a number of objects and write a simple text for the picture. (Either allow children to choose or assign the number of objects from one to ten.) Combine pictures with text into a group-made book.

Lyon, George Ella. **Counting on the Woods**. New York: DK, 1998. Unpaged. Photographs by Ann W. Olson. $15.95. ISBN 0-7894-2480-0.

- ■ PICTURE BOOK—Concept Book
- ■ Ages 3–7

Summary

Full-page color photos taken in the eastern Kentucky Appalachian woodlands provide the backdrop for a simple one-to-ten counting rhyme that identifies details in the photos.

Bookwalk/Read-Aloud

"Simply look and wonders will appear" (quote the book jacket). What will we see if we walk along the path with the boy? Let's find out. We will see two birds, three bugs, four worms, five nests, six tracks, seven stones, eight flowers, nine vines, and ten trees. Introduce this book with a Bookwalk, then read aloud and show the pictures.

Curriculum Connections

Take the children outside (e.g., to the library grounds, the school yard, a home yard, or a neighborhood) to explore the natural environment. Talk about what they see, then with a disposable camera, have them each take one picture of the natural environment. (Or teachers can take pictures with children directing them as to what to photograph.) Develop the pictures. Have students identify and count details in the pictures, and write a simple text. Using *Counting on the Woods* as a model, have students put together student-made photo books.

Related Books

Another book that focuses on looking at the natural environment is *Out of the Ocean* by Debra Frasier. It is reviewed in this chapter under "Ecosystems."

MacDonald, Suse. **Look Who's Counting**. New York: Scholastic Press, 2000. Unpaged. $14.95. ISBN 0-590-68320-9.

■ **PICTURE BOOK—Concept Book**
■ **AGES 3–7**

Summary

Owl counts what she sees as she flies through the night. The text uses numerals that are repeated as part of the illustration. The left page introduces the new number while the right page shows the cumulative numbers and repeats the line: "She counted" ("She counted 1." "She counted 1, 2," and so on).

Bookwalk/Read-Aloud

(Show the book to the children as you talk.) Owl has just learned to count. As she flies through the night she counts what she sees: one prairie dog, two mice, three ducks, four moths, five cranes, six sheep, seven bats, eight spiders, nine squirrels, and ten snails. Read aloud and use for repeated readings.

Curriculum Connections

On repeated readings encourage children to chime in with the counting especially the line "She counted . . .". Give each child a set of numbers from one to ten. As they listen to you read, have them select and hold up the appropriate number for each page. Talk with the children about the number of objects they see in the room (e.g., five children, three books, two plants). Using the book as a model, have children draw pictures of the objects they see using numbers as part of the illustrations. Title the pictures "I see (number, object)."

Schnur, Steven. **Night Lights**. New York: Farrar, Straus & Giroux, 2000. Unpaged. Illustrated by Stacey Schuett. $16.00. ISBN 0-374-35522-3.

■ **PICTURE BOOK—Concept Book**
■ **AGES 3–7**

Summary

At bedtime, a little girl counts the lights she sees beginning with the lights in her room, then the lights outside her window—along the street, in the distance, and in the sky. She counts from one to twenty, then fifty, one hundred, one thousand, and one million.

Booktalk/Bookwalk

Melinda counted the lights that she saw before she went to bed. In her bedroom, she saw one night-light, two blinking clocks, three burning logs, and four candles. When she looked out her window she saw five TV sets, six lanterns, seven fireflies, and eight lighted windows. As she looked up and down the street she counted even more lights. Then she looked up to the sky. Now she was no longer able to count, but could only imagine. What might you see if you counted the lights before you went to bed?

Curriculum Connections

You may wish to use this book to introduce counting from one to twenty and beyond to fifty, one hundred, one thousand, and finally one million. Because this book begins with what is near and gradually looks farther and farther away, you might also use it with older children as a descriptive writing model that begins by describing what is near and then systematically describes what is farther and farther away.

Fractions

Pinczes, Elinor J. **Inchworm and a Half.** Boston: Houghton Mifflin, 2001. Unpaged. Illustrated by Randall Enos. $15.00. ISBN 0-395-82849-X.

■ **PICTURE BOOK—Verse**
■ **AGES 7–10**

Summary

Rhyming verse accompanies the illustrations showing the inchworm, half-inchworm, one-third-inchworm, and one-fourth-inchworm measuring their world of leaves and vegetables.

Read-Aloud

Introduce the book by telling children to listen carefully so they can help the inchworm. Then read aloud showing the pictures. Pause in the middle of page 7 after the question, "What's nearly three?" and ask the children to answer the question. Continue reading to page 18. Pause and ask the children to answer the question, "What length could it possibly be?" Read to page 27. Pause and ask the children to answer the question, then read to the end of the book.

Curriculum Connections

Use this book to review and practice fractions. Read the book after children have been introduced to fractions, in particular, one-half, one-third, and one-fourth. Follow up by having children draw, color, and cut out inchworms that are one-half, one-third, and one-fourth inches in length. Then have the children use the inchworms to measure objects in the room such as pens, paper, books, or crayons.

Related Books

Other books by Elinor Pinczes are *A Remainder of One*, *One Hundred Hungry Ants*, and *Arctic Fives Arrive*.

Geometric Shapes

Dotlich, Rebecca Kai. **What Is a Triangle?** New York: Harper-Festival, 2000. Unpaged. Photographs by Maria Ferrari. $9.95. ISBN 0-694-01392-7.

■ **PICTURE BOOK—Concept Book; Triangles**
■ **AGES 3–7**

Summary

Simple photographs, one per page, show real-life, triangular objects such as an ice-cream cone, a birthday hat, and a boat with a sail. Simple text, two lines per page, identifies each real-life object.

Bookwalk/Read-Aloud

Turn the pages, show the pictures, and name the objects on each page.

Curriculum Connections

Prepare by placing triangular real-life objects in your library, media center, or classroom. Introduce the book and the concept of triangles with concrete items that are triangles such as the rhythm band triangle, a building block, or Lego™ piece. Talk about triangles, then take a picture walk through the book. Follow up by looking for triangular real-life objects in your immediate environment (library, media center, classroom).

Hoban, Tana. **Cubes, Cones, Cylinders & Spheres**. New York: Greenwillow Books, 2000. Unpaged. $15.95. ISBN 0-688-15325-9.

- ■ **PICTURE BOOK—Concept Book**
- ■ **AGES 3–7**

Summary

This is a wordless book with photographs, one per page, that show real-life objects such as building blocks, ice-cream cones, and a hot-air balloon that are cubes, cones, cylinders, and spheres.

Bookwalk

Turn the pages and show the pictures having the children name the objects on each page. Encourage some discussion of the objects as you go through the book.

Curriculum Connections

Introduce the book and the concepts of cubes, cones, cylinders, and spheres using building blocks. Allow the children to handle the blocks and talk about and name them. Ask: What makes a cube a cube? Or a cone a cone? Then take a picture walk through the book. Follow up by looking for cubes, cones, cylinders, and spheres in your immediate environment (library, media center, or classroom).

Percentages

Pallotta, Jerry. **Twizzlers™ Pecentages Book**. New York: Scholastic Press, 2001. Unpaged. Illustrated by Rob Bolster. $10.95. ISBN 0-439-25407-8.

- ■ **PICTURE BOOK**
- ■ **AGES 7–12**

Summary

The mini-spaceship on the teacher's desk promises to teach the class about percentages in return for Twizzlers™ Twists candy. Full-page illustrations of candy, the spaceship, fractions, and percentages with accompanying text develop the concept and calculation of percentages.

Bookwalk

Introduce the book by showing the pictures and telling the children about each two-page spread. The first two-page spread reviews math symbols; the next shows 100 percent. Then base ten and place value are explained. Next 90 percent and 10 percent are shown. The next four two-page spreads show different patterns and different percentages. Problems to solve follow on the next two two-page spreads. Next comes changing a percent to a fraction. Finally, decimals and rounding off are explained.

Curriculum Connections

Use this book to review and practice percentages. Give the children concrete objects, such as candy, tongue depressors, or counting chips. Have the children re-create with their objects the patterns and problems presented in the book.

Probability

Axelrod, Amy. **Pigs at Odds: Fun with Math and Games**. New York: Simon & Schuster, 2000. Unpaged. Illustrated by Sharon McGinley-Nally. $14.00. ISBN 0-689-81566-2.

■ **PICTURE BOOK**
■ **AGES 4–9**

Summary

The seventh in a series of books about the Pig Family and mathematics, this book takes the Pig Family to the county fair where they play games and win prizes. The focus is on probability with explanations and problems to solve at the beginning and end of the book.

Booktalk

Have you ever been to a fair? The Pig Family went to the county fair. First, they had fun on the rides. Then they went to play the games. Sometimes they won. Sometimes they lost. Were the games fair? Did the pigs need to practice in order the win the prizes? Did you ever play games at a fair or carnival?

Curriculum Connections

Introduce, develop, or review the concept of probability with this book. Young children will enjoy the detailed and lively cartoon-like illustrations that lend themselves to discussion and oral language development. Older children will enjoy the problems to solve, such as: Which games depend on luck? Which games depend on skill? What is the probability that the spinner will land on November? Read aloud, focus attention on the illustrations, and provide opportunities to revisit the text.

Related Books

Other books about the Pig Family and mathematics listed on the back cover of the book are: *Pigs Will Be Pigs: Fun with Math and Money*, *Pigs on a Blanket: Fun with Math and Time*, *Pigs in the Pantry: Fun with Math and Cooking*, *Pigs Go to Market: Fun with Math and Shopping*, *Pigs on the Ball: Fun with Math and Sports*, and *Pigs on the Move: Fun with Math and Travel*.

Problem Solving

Daniels, Teri. **Math Man**. New York: Orchard Books, 2001. Unpaged. Illustrated by Timothy Bush. $16.95. ISBN 0-439-29308-1.

■ **PICTURE BOOK**
■ **AGES 7 and up**

Summary

Mrs. Gourd takes her class to the Mighty Mart to see math in action. Garth the stock boy is the math man who has a way with numbers. Watch for the mouse family tucked into the illustrations.

Booktalk

What can you tell Mr. Pit when a whole watermelon is too big to fit in the refrigerator? What could you say to the mom who is buying a box of four treats for her five children? Marnie needs help too. She has a dollar and wants to buy a pumpkin. Garth the stock boy is the math man who can help. Can you help too?

Curriculum Connections

Have children help Garth the stock boy solve the math problems in the book (e.g., count by twos and then by tens, calculate the price of pumpkins at forty cents per pound, and add the grocery orders at the checkout counter). Follow up by having children create their own grocery story math problems to solve.

Ratio and Proportion

Schwartz, David M. **If You Hopped Like a Frog**. New York: Scholastic Press, 1999. Unpaged. $15.95. ISBN 0-590-09857-8.

- ■ **PICTURE BOOK—Concept Book**
- ■ **AGES 5–9**

Summary

The author introduces and develops ratio and proportion with statements such as: "If you hopped like a frog, you could jump to home plate from first base in one mighty leap!" The last four pages elaborate on each statement with additional information and pose a word problem for children to solve.

Bookwalk

Introduce the book by showing the children the illustration and reading "If you hopped like a frog," and ask, "Then what would happen?" Encourage children to predict the answer then read the next page. After the first three, "If you hopped like a frog," "If you were as strong as an ant," and "If you had the brain of a Brachiosaurus," turn to the page that says "If you had eagle eyes" and ask for predictions, but leave them hanging by saying, "You'll have to read to find out!"

Curriculum Connections

Use this book to encourage predictions and to stimulate the creation of and the solutions to word problems. Have children create additional scenarios for each "If you were . . .". Solve the word problems in the back of the book and then have children use the information to create additional word problems for friends or classmates to solve.

Riddles

Tang, Greg. **The Grapes of Math**. New York: Scholastic Press, 2001. Unpaged. Illustrated by Harry Briggs. $16.95. ISBN 0-439-21033-X.

- ■ **PICTURE BOOK**
- ■ **ALL AGES**

Summary

Computer-generated illustrations and sixteen rhyming riddles challenge readers to create groups and then add and subtract to find the answers. The riddles develop problem solving by encouraging readers to look beyond the obvious, to think strategically, to organize information by identifying patterns and symmetries, and to use a variety of skills such as adding and subtracting. Solutions to the riddles and an "Author's Note" are in the back of the book.

Booktalk/Bookwalk

Now put on your thinking caps and to get ready to listen because I have a riddle for you to solve. One way to solve the riddle is by counting, but counting is slow. A faster way to solve the riddle is to look for patterns and then to add and subtract. (Begin with the first riddle. Be sure to show the illustration as you read the riddle.)

Curriculum Connections

Use this book to introduce or to review and practice grouping and identification of patterns and symmetries. Illustrations may also be used to introduce the concepts or as examples of tessellations. Although the book focuses on adding and subtracting, multiplying and dividing may also be used to solve the riddles. Extend the book by encouraging children to create their own riddles with illustrations.

Thompson, Lauren. **One Riddle, One Answer.** New York: Scholastic Press, 2001. Unpaged. Illustrated by Linda S. Wingerter. $15.95. ISBN 0-590-31335-5.

■ **PICTURE BOOK**
■ **AGES 7 and up**

Summary

Azziza, the daughter of the Persian sultan, loves numbers and riddles. When it is time for her to marry, she poses a riddle for her suitors to answer. The man who answers the riddle will become her husband. Clues to the riddle are in the story. The solution to the riddle is explained on the last two pages of the book.

Booktalk

Begin by presenting the riddle to the children. Encourage attempts to solve the riddle. Then tell the children that this is the riddle that Azziza, the daughter of the Persian sultan, presented to her suitors. The man who answered the riddle would become her husband. Clues to the riddle are in the story.

Curriculum Connections

Have children listen for clues as you read aloud or as they read the book silently. Have them record the clues and attempt to solve the riddle. Check their solutions against the solution in the back of the book. Test the solutions against the four parts of the riddle.

Time

Jones, Carol. **What's the Time, Mr. Wolf?** Boston: Houghton Mifflin, 1999. Unpaged. $15.00. ISBN 0-395-95800-8.

■ **PICTURE BOOK**
■ **AGES 3–8**

Summary

Mr. Wolf plans a very special meal. As his barnyard friends ask him for the time at two-hour intervals throughout the day, Mr. Wolf tells them the time, and then sends them off for such items as a cookbook, mint sauce, and oranges. Each two-page spread has a round hole in the page that previews the next illustration and frames the recurring question "What's the time, Mr. Wolf?"

Booktalk/Bookwalk

One day, Mr. Wolf decided to have a very special meal. When rooster woke him at 8:00 A.M. by asking, "What's the time, Mr. Wolf?" Mr. Wolf sent him off for a cookbook. At 10:00 A.M. when donkey asked, "What's the time, Mr. Wolf?" Mr. Wolf sent him off for a bottle of tomato sauce. At 12:00 P.M. sheep asked (encourage children to repeat the question) "What's the time, Mr. Wolf?" Mr. Wolf sent him off for a bottle of mint sauce. At 2:00 and then 4:00 P.M., cow and then pig asked (encourage children to repeat the question). What do you think Mr. Wolf did? (Encourage predictions.) Finally, at 6:00 P.M., Mr. Wolf announced that it was time for the party to begin. What do you think happened at the party? (Encourage more predictions.)

Curriculum Connections

Use in conjunction with the development of time concepts, particularly recognizing the hour and two-hour intervals. Use for readers' theater with children playing the roles of Mr. Wolf and the barnyard animals.

Related Books

Another book that develops concepts of time is *Game Time!* by Stuart J. Murphy. It is reviewed in this section.

Murphy, Stuart J. **Game Time!** New York: HarperTrophy, 2000. 33p. Illustrated by Cynthia Jabar. $4.95. ISBN 0-06-446732-5.

■ **PICTURE BOOK**
■ **AGES 7 and up**

Summary

Concepts about time such as the months, weeks, days, hours, minutes, and seconds are skillfully woven into the story about the big soccer game between the Falcons and the Huskies. Other mathematics concepts such as counting and game scores are included. Time facts are illustrated at the back of the book.

Booktalk/Bookwalk

Introduce the book by retelling the story while turning pages and focusing on the time concepts presented in the illustrations. Begin by repeating the countdown chant exchanged between the two teams. On the next page call attention to the clock and calendar in the illustration. Tell children that the big game will be played on October 14. Because it is already 2:00 on October 7, the game is only one week away. The teams have only seven more days to practice. Turn the page, point to the clock and the calendar, and say that the teams practiced all week. Now it is 11:15 A.M. on Friday. The game is only one day away. Rebecca tells her friend Ashley that in twenty-four hours the game will be over. Turn the page and show children the scoreboard and the clock. Tell the children that it is 9:00. The teams have one hour to warm up. In sixty minutes the soccer game will begin. Until then, the score is zero to zero. Continue in this manner with each page until the end when you can invite the children to cheer with the winning team.

Curriculum Connections

Suggested activities for responding to the book and developing concepts of time (e.g., making a list of the ways in which time is measured or listing four events that happened in a day and drawing four clocks showing the time for each event) are included at the back of the book. Have children make up other activities that require converting time periods from months to weeks to days, hours, minutes, and seconds.

Related Books

Other books that introduce and develop concepts of time are *What's the Time, Mr. Wolf?* by Carol Jones, which is reviewed in this section, and three books suggested by the author: *The Grouchy Ladybug* by Eric Carle, *Time To . . .* by Bruce Macmillan, and *Tuesday* by David Wiesner. Other books in the MathStart Series are *Let's Fly a Kite* about symmetry and *Monster Musical Chairs* about subtracting one.

SCIENCE

Critters

Arnold, Caroline. **Australian Animals**. New York: HarperCollins, 2000. 48p. $15.95. ISBN 0-688-16766-7.

- ■ **PICTURE BOOK—Nonfiction**
- ■ **AGES 5 and up**

Summary

A two-page spread with colored photographs and a two-paragraph description introduce readers to seventeen animals, birds, snakes, and lizards of Australia.

Bookwalk

Introduce the book by showing the photographs and naming the animals, birds, snakes, and lizards. Encourage children to repeat the names.

Curriculum Connections

Create a zookeeper's chart of Australian animals. Make four columns with the following headings: Student's Name, Animal, Place Animal Lives, and Animal Eats. Have each child fill in one line of the chart then create a shoe box diorama of the animal's cage, showing the animal in its habitat. Label each diorama with the name of the animal, its locale (forest and woodlands, grasslands, desert, or water's edge), and a short description of its habitat. Set up a display of shoe box dioramas.

Related Books

Caroline Arnold has written similar books about animals in other parts of the world titled *African Animals* and *South American Animals*.

Arnosky, Jim. **All About Turtles**. New York: Scholastic Press, 2000. Unpaged. $15.95. ISBN 0-590-48145-5.

- ■ **PICTURE BOOK—Nonfiction**
- ■ **AGES 5 and up**

Summary

Full-color illustrations, labels, captions, and informative, simple text introduce readers to the world of turtles.

Booktalk/Bookwalk

(Introduce this book with the five questions that the author uses.) "Have you ever wondered about turtles? How many kinds of turtles are there? Why do turtles have shells? What do turtles eat? How old can turtles live to be?" (Engage children in a discussion of these questions. Show pages 5–6.) Tell the children, "Here we see pictures of different kinds of turtles." (Turn to pages 7–8.) Tell the children, "Here we see the top and bottom view of a turtle shell." (Turn to pages 13–14.) "Here's what turtles eat."

Curriculum Connections

Use this book in conjunction with a study of turtles or of the natural environment. Identify the turtles that live in the environment you are studying. Extend the book by visiting a turtle Web site such as the Leatherback Turtle Working Group at http://www.seaturtle.ca. Compare and contrast the different kinds of turtles you studied by creating a semantic feature analysis chart (see Appendix A).

Bouchard, David. **A Barnyard Bestiary**. Custer, WA: Orca, 1999. Unpaged. Illustrated by Kimball Allen. $14.95. ISBN 1-55143-131-9.

- ■ **PICTURE BOOK—Poetry**
- ■ **AGES 10 and up**

Summary

Twelve animals such as the buffalo, donkey, sheep, and turkey speak in first-person verse of their relationships with man.

Booktalk

In this book, familiar animals talk to you about their experiences with humans, some good and some not so good. The buffalo is bitter while the Shire horse is proud of his heritage. The ostrich is hopeful while the Border collie continues to be man's loyal friend. The turkey, donkey, and goose also speak. What do you suppose they have to say?

Curriculum Connections

The unifying theme of this collection is the relationship between the animals and man. Use these poems in conjunction with a study of interrelationships, of man and his environment, and of concepts about land use and stewardship.

Bunting, Eve. **The Butterfly House**. New York: Scholastic Press, 1999. Unpaged. Illustrated by Greg Shed. $15.95. ISBN 0-590-84884-4.

- **PICTURE BOOK—Fiction**
- **AGES 5–12**

Summary

A young girl and her grandfather make a butterfly house for a larva that will emerge as a butterfly. This charming intergenerational book uses first-person narrative with soft illustrations to accompany each page of text. Instructions for building a butterfly house and raising a butterfly are given at the end of the book.

Booktalk

What kind of a house do you suppose a butterfly lives in? This is a story about a girl who found a butterfly larva. With her grandfather, she made a butterfly house using a small covered box. Do you suppose the larva really turned into a butterfly inside the covered box? What do you think happened?

Curriculum Connections

Introduce children to the lyrical language and delicate illustrations of this charming intergenerational story by reading aloud and showing the pictures as each page is read. Use this book in conjunction with a butterfly garden or a nature unit. Follow instructions in the back of the book to build a butterfly house and raise a butterfly. Provide the children with boxes about one square foot in size, such as shoe boxes with lids, and paper, colors, or paints. Encourage them to decorate their boxes using a lot of green and brown just like the little girl did in the book.

Cowley, Joy. **Red-Eyed Tree Frog**. New York: Scholastic Press, 1999. Unpaged. Photographs by Nic Bishop. $16.95. ISBN 0-590-87175-7.

- ■ **PICTURE BOOK—Nonfiction**
- ■ **AGES 5 and up**

Summary

Color photographs and simple text introduce the tree frog waking up hungry as evening falls in the rain forest. The reader follows the tree frog as he finds something to eat and then falls asleep when morning comes. Two pages at the end of the book add information about what frogs do and do not eat and why, and what creatures eat frogs.

Bookwalk/Read-Aloud

This is a book to be read aloud and shown with its artful photographs and sparse text.

Curriculum Connections

Discuss with the children what frogs do and do not eat, and what might eat a frog. Brainstorm a list based on the text and what children know. Add information from the back of the book. Create a chart with three columns and use the three headings: What Frogs Eat, What Frogs Do Not Eat, and What Eats Frogs.

Galvin, Laura Gates. **Deer Mouse at Old Farm Road**. Norwalk, CT: Soundprints, 1998. Unpaged. $19.95. ISBN 1-568-99517-2.

- ■ **PICTURE BOOK—Fiction**
- ■ **AGES 3–8**

Summary

Deer Mouse prepares a nest for her new babies that are born the next morning. Brilliant, full-page illustrations augment the text. The book concludes with a brief description of deer mice and a glossary. A unique concluding feature of this book is the section "Points of Interest," which identifies details of the illustrations, such as downy woodpecker feathers, mulberries, and dandelion down.

Booktalk

It is mid-July and Deer Mouse is preparing a nest for her new babies. In the black of night she leaves her nest to forage for food. As she finishes her midnight snack, Deer Mouse hears a sound, sees the leaves on a bush move slightly, and knows that something is hiding. She lets out a shrill cry and thumps her feet before running to the safety of a hole in a nearby stone wall. A cat is in close pursuit! How will Deer Mouse finish her nest? What will happen to her babies?

Curriculum Connections

Re-create the environment that Deer Mouse lives in. Have children gather natural materials such as sticks and leaves from outdoors, then make a collage showing Deer Mouse's habitat.

Related Books

Another book by Laura Gates Galvin is *Armadillo at Riverside Road* also from Soundprints. Contact Soundprints at 353 Main Avenue, Norwalk, CT 06851 or at http://www.soundprints.com for companion read-along audiocassettes, stuffed animal toys, multimedia interactive presentations, and interactive storybooks.

High, Linda Oatman. **Beekeepers.** Honesdale, PA: Boyds Mills Press, 1998. Unpaged. $14.95. ISBN 1-56397-486-X.

- **PICTURE BOOK—Fiction**
- **AGES 5–9**

Summary

A young girl and her grandfather tend honeybees. Full-page impressionistic oil paintings illustrate the poetic text to produce another gentle intergenerational story.

Booktalk

Have you ever been stung by a bee? Have you ever seen a bee-hive? Did you know that beekeepers sometimes have to move a whole swarm of bees? Here's a story about a girl who helps her grandfather tend honeybees. How would you feel about doing that?

Curriculum Connections

Encourage children to learn more about bees by developing a K-W-L (What do we Know? What do we Want to know? What have we Learned?) chart. Stimulate additional interest by serving samples of different kinds of honey (e.g., orange blossom honey, clover honey, local area honey, generic honey).

Lewin, Ted. **Nilo and the Tortoise**. New York: Scholastic Press, 1999. Unpaged. $16.95. ISBN 0-590-96004-0.

- **PICTURE BOOK—Fiction**
- **AGES 5–10**

Summary

This is a semiautobiographical story in which the author retells an adventure that he had on the Galapagos Islands. In the story, the boy Nilo is stranded overnight on an island when the anchor line breaks and his father's boat is swept out to sea with an engine in need of repair. Nilo comes face-to-face with the island creatures and sleeps through the night with a tortoise.

Booktalk

Have you ever been stranded? Nilo was. He and his father anchored near an island so that his father could repair the engine on his boat. Nilo was allowed to go ashore while his father worked. After Nilo played along the shore, he returned to the beach to find that the anchor line had broken and his father's boat had been swept out to sea. Nilo knew that it would be a while before his father could repair the engine and come back for him. So he set out to explore the island. He didn't know there were angry sea lions and even a volcano on the island.

Curriculum Connections

Find the Galapagos Islands on a world map. The last two pages of the book give information about the creatures that Nilo encountered and name other creatures found on the islands and in the surrounding waters. Have students research additional information about the Galapagos Islands and the creatures that live there.

McNulty, Faith. **How Whales Walked into the Sea**. New York: Scholastic Press, 1999. Unpaged. Illustrated by Ted Rand. $16.95. ISBN 0-590-89830-2.

■ **PICTURE BOOK—Nonfiction**
■ **ALL AGES**

Summary

Chalk, acrylic, and watercolor paintings and a narrative text tell the story of how whales evolved from large, furry, land animals.

Booktalk

Have you ever heard of a Mesonychid? What do you think it was? The Mesonychid lived more than thirty million years ago. He was a furry, four-legged animal that hunted other animals and caught fish. But eventually, it learned to swim, and became better suited to live in the water than on land. Then it evolved into another creature, and yet another. What do you think those were?

Curriculum Connections

Create a time line showing the evolution of whales. Have students try to image thirty million years. How many children are in your school? How many people are in your city?

Mead, Alice. **Billy and Emma**. New York: Farrar, Straus & Giroux, 2000. Unpaged. Illustrated by Christy Hale. $16.00. ISBN 0-374-30705-9.

■ **PICTURE BOOK—Fiction**
■ **AGES 3–8**

Summary

When a robber steals Emma the macaw from her cage at the zoo, her friends Billy, another macaw, and Nancy the crow find her with the help of some pigeons and bring her back to the zoo.

Booktalk

If it hadn't been for the pigeons, Billy and Nancy might never have found Emma. Billy and Emma were best friends who lived together in a cage at the Willowby Zoo. They were macaws. Do you know what a macaw is? (Invite children to answer.) Three times a day Billy and Emma put on a show for visitors to the zoo. One night when only Harold the owl was awake, a robber slipped into the zoo, cut the wires of the cage where Billy and Emma lived, and stole Emma. Later when Emma had still not returned and no one could find her, Harold the owl helped Billy escape from his cage. Billy and Nancy the crow searched the city all night long. By morning they had not found Emma. Not only that, they were hopelessly lost. What could they do?

Curriculum Connections

Use this book as an introduction to a study of birds. The "Author's Note" at the end of the book gives information about the birds that are in the book: macaws, owls, crows, flamingos, and pigeons. Ask the children if any of them have birds as pets. Invite them to tell the group about their pet birds. Encourage questions and discussion about birds. Ask the children to brainstorm a list of birds that they would like to know more about. Group the children into pairs or teams of four depending on the size of your group. Have each pair or team research a bird of interest to them and report on it—its size, color, where it lives, what it eats, how many there are, and so on.

Simon, Seymour. **Gorillas**. New York: HarperCollins, 2000. Unpaged. $15.95. ISBN 0-06-023035-5.

■ **PICTURE BOOK—Nonfiction**
■ **AGES 5–8**

Summary

Full-color photographs and informative text introduce readers to different kinds of gorillas, how they gather food, how they live in family groups of adults and children, and how they communicate and play.

Booktalk

Do you think gorillas are scary? Actually, they're very shy animals. What do you already know about gorillas? (Stop and list what the children know about gorillas then continue.) There's more to learn about gorillas: All of them live in heavily forested areas of Africa. There are three groups or subspecies of gorillas: western lowland gorillas, eastern lowland gorillas, and mountain gorillas. This book shows you how gorillas live, communicate, think, and feel.

Curriculum Connections

With the children, create a semantic feature analysis chart that identifies attributes of the three subgroups of gorillas that are identified in the book.

Swope, Sam. **Gotta Go! Gotta Go!** New York: Farrar, Straus & Giroux, 2000. Unpaged. Illustrated by Sue Riddle. $12.00. ISBN 0-374-32757-2.

■ **PICTURE BOOK**
■ **AGES 3–8**

Summary

The creepy-crawly bug crawls out of its egg in the meadow, turns into a monarch butterfly, flies to Mexico, then returns to the meadow to lay eggs.

Read-Aloud

Read aloud so that children can hear, enjoy, and mimic the repetitive language used in this book.

Curriculum Connections

Visit a butterfly garden, identify the different kinds of butterflies, and learn about the monarch butterfly. Find Mexico on the map, trace the route, and calculate how far the monarch butterfly must fly from your community. Read the book, then create a readers' theater script with the children. Have the children give a readers' theater performance based on this book.

Ecosystems

Bial, Raymond. **A Handful of Dirt**. New York: Walker, 2000. 32p. $16.95. ISBN 0-8027-8698-7.

- ■ **PICTURE BOOK—Nonfiction**
- ■ **AGES 8–12**

Summary

Color photographs illustrate the text that explains the composition and creation of soil as a continuous cycle of life, death, and decay.

Booktalk

Does your mom ever tell you not to get dirty, or scold you when you come home with dirty clothes? (Have the children respond verbally or by raising their hands.) Did you know that there would be no life on Earth without dirt? Did you ever wonder where dirt came from? *A Handful of Dirt* (show book) explains how rocks, plants, and animals break down into the soil in which fruits, vegetables, grasses, and grains grow to feed the animals and us.

Curriculum Connections

Give the children an opportunity to experience the soil that the book explains. Take them outside. Have each child dig up a handful of dirt, place it in a container, and then sift through it looking for bugs, debris, and pieces of organic matter. Give each child a magnifying glass to better see what is in his or her dirt. Take the children inside. Allow them to examine their dirt under a microscope. Have them talk about and then make a chart of what they see using the following headings: With the Naked Eye, With a Magnifying Glass, and Under a Microscope. If you are gardening with children, start a compost pile and use the compost in your garden.

Cherry, Lynne, and Mark J. Plotkin. **The Shaman's Apprentice**. New York: Harcourt Brace, 1998. Unpaged. $6.00. ISBN 0-15-201281-8.

■ **PICTURE BOOK—Fiction; Multicultural; Native Americans**
■ **AGES 6 and up**

Summary

Deep, brilliant, full-page, watercolor paintings illustrate the boxed text that tells of the young boy, Kamanya, who is cured of his illness by the medicine man, Natahlah, and then grows up to become Natahlah's apprentice. Set in the Amazon rain forest, this story is based on the true story of the Tirio tribe who discovered the importance of their traditional plant medicines.

Bookwalk

Introduce this book to the children by showing the pictures and briefly retelling the story of Kamanya. Be sure to point out Natahlah's use of traditional plant medicines.

Curriculum Connections

Follow up by showing the video, *The Shaman's Apprentice: A Tale of the Amazon Rain Forest*, which is available from Reading Rainbow. Use this book and video in conjunction with a study of the rain forest. Include concepts of sustainability and ethnobiology (man's effect on the environment), both of which are introduced by the book and video. Mark Plotkin further develops the concepts in his book that is cited below in "Related Books."

Related Books

The Shaman's Apprentice is based on Mark Plotkin's *Tales of the Shaman's Apprentice* in which the author, who is an ethnobiologist, tells of his experiences studying the traditional plant medicines of the Tirio tribe in the Amazon rain forest. *Tales of the Shaman's Apprentice* is written for adults and is likely to appeal to capable readers who want to know more about the topic.

Fleischman, Paul. **Weslandia**. Cambridge, MA: Candlewick Press, 1999. Unpaged. Illustrated by Kevin Hawkes. $15.99. ISBN 0-7636-0006-7.

- ■ **PICTURE BOOK—Fiction**
- ■ **AGES 7–12**

Summary

Wesley, the class outcast, develops a sustainable environment in his own backyard and becomes the most popular kid in his class. Lively, colorful illustrations supplement the text and stimulate the imagination.

Booktalk

Do you ever feel like an outcast? Wesley does. He doesn't like pizza, soda pop, football, or the haircuts that other boys wear. Even his parents think he's odd. Maybe Wesley needs his own civilization. Then maybe, just maybe, he'll become the most popular kid in class.

Curriculum Connection

This book is a good choice to explore the topic of sustainability. Look at your own natural environment and consider how it influences daily life. Raise questions about the natural environment and how people use what they find to meet their needs. What does your natural environment provide? How is it used? Encourage children to brainstorm ideas for improving their community by better using the natural environment.

Related Books

Swiss Family Robinson and Robinson Crusoe are two books in which the characters create sustainable environments for themselves. The Shaman's Apprentice, which is reviewed in this section, also addresses the topic of using the natural environment to meet one's needs.

Frasier, Debra. **Out of the Ocean**. New York: Harcourt Brace, 1998. Unpaged. $16.00. ISBN 0-15-258849-3.

■ **PICTURE BOOK**
■ **AGES 3 and up**

Summary

Collage illustrations, photographs, and text show the reader gifts that the ocean provides. Different native plants border each page. The text is written in dialogue between mother and child with the mother saying, "You can ask the ocean to bring you something." The mother explains that she asks for the sun, water, shells, and treasures, and that she always finds what she asks for. We discover with the child that the secret is in the looking rather than the asking. The book ends with a six page journal of text and photos that provide a glossary of items that one might find along the shore.

Booktalk/Bookwalk

Introduce children to this book by telling the children that the mother said, "You can ask the ocean to bring you something." Show and talk about the pictures and text on each page. Name what the mother asks for (e.g., the sun, water, shells, and other treasures). Be sure to call attention to the native plants that border each page.

Curriculum Connections

Engage children in a conversation about what might be found along the shore, at the beach, or along a riverbank. Make lists, draw pictures, make a collage, or set up a display of items. Have children research an ocean creature and make a report. Children may create their own book of treasures using this book as a model.

Related Books

Another book that focuses on looking at the natural environment is *Counting on the Woods* by George Ella Lyon. It is reviewed in this chapter under "Mathematics."

Hunter, Anne. **What's in the Pond?** New York: Houghton Mifflin, 1999. Unpaged. $4.95. ISBN 0-395-91224-5.

- **PICTURE BOOK—Nonfiction**
- **AGES 3–7**

Summary

A little book, just the right size for little hands, introduces young readers to the damselfly, bluegill, red-winged blackbird, frog, turtle, and other critters who live in, on, or near the pond.

Bookwalk

Show the pictures and name each critter. Have children repeat each name.

Curriculum Connections

Have children create a mural showing life in the pond. Have each child draw, color, cut out, write the name, and paste a critter in its appropriate spot in the pond.

Related Books

A similar book by Anne Hunter is *What's on the Log?*

Markle, Sandra. **Down, Down, Down in the Ocean**. New York: Walker, 1999. 32p. $16.95. ISBN 0-80-27-8654-5.

- **PICTURE BOOK—Nonfiction**
- **AGES 7–12**

Summary

This book explores the Pacific Ocean ecosystem off the coast of California at 0–200 meters, 200–1,000 meters, and 1,000 meters.

Booktalk/Bookwalk

What can you see beneath the surface of the ocean? *Down, Down, Down in the Ocean* (show book) takes us on a journey into the Pacific Ocean. You'll go deeper and deeper from 0 to 200 meters, where you might see a shark (turn page), tiny green plants called algae, microscopic and tiny worms (turn page), a school of herring and a salmon, a shark pup (turn page), and a seal. From 200 to 1,000 meters you might see an eel (turn page), a silver hatchet fish (turn page), a salp (turn page), and a whale and a squid. On the ocean bottom at 1,000 meters you might see jellylike creatures (turn page), a gulper eel and prawn (turn page), and an anglerfish (turn page). Finally, the seafloor is muddy (turn page) and is a home for clams, crabs, eelpouts, and tube worms.

Curriculum Connections

Make drawings or shoe box dioramas of the ocean depths: 0–200 meters, 200–1,000 meters, 1,000 meters—the ocean bottom, the seafloor.

Related Books

Other books by Sandra Markle are *After the Spill, Super Cool Science*, and *Creepy, Crawly Baby Bugs*.

Morrison, Gordon. **Oak Tree**. Boston: Houghton Mifflin, 2000. 30p. $16.00. ISBN 0-395-95644-7.

■ **PICTURE BOOK—Nonfiction**
■ **AGES 5–12**

Summary

The reader follows the oak tree and its inhabitants (squirrels, birds, caterpillars, butterflies, honeybees, and others) through the changes of the seasons from winter to spring, summer, fall, and the return of winter.

Bookwalk

Show the book, turn the pages, and talk about the signs of life that you see in or on the oak tree on each page.

Curriculum Connections

Talk with the children about what they already know about oak trees. Select an oak tree in your immediate environment. Select another kind of tree if you do not have an oak tree. Observe the tree regularly and record the signs of life that you see living in or on the tree.

Engineering

Curlee, Lynn. **Rushmore**. New York: Scholastic Press, 1999. 48p. $17.95. ISBN 0-590-22573-1.

- ■ **PICTURE BOOK**
- ■ **AGES 8 and up**

Summary

This is a nontraditional picture book (intended for fluent rather than beginning readers) that recounts the carving of Mount Rushmore in the Black Hills of South Dakota. Mount Rushmore was named in 1885 for the young lawyer who worked for the mining company that owned tin mines in the Black Hills of South Dakota. Between 1927 and 1941, four famous faces were carved into the side of the mountain. Mount Rushmore National Memorial honors George Washington, Thomas Jefferson, Abraham Lincoln, and Theodore Roosevelt, and is called "The Shrine of Democracy."

Booktalk/Bookwalk

(Show the cover of the book as you begin the booktalk.) Dynamite and jackhammers, an aerial cable tram, a wooden stairway with platforms and ramps, hand winches, cables, and sling seats were the tools that helped workmen to carve the faces of George Washington, Thomas Jefferson, Abraham Lincoln, and Teddy Roosevelt into the side of Mount Rushmore in the Black Hills of South Dakota.

(Show the two-page illustration on the title page then show the map on page 9. Continue the booktalk.) There were decisions to be made about the figures to be carved, then problems to be solved, and money to be raised. (Show the two-page illustration on pages 34–35.)

(Conclude the booktalk.) John Gutzon de la Mothe Borglum, the sculptor who carved Stone Mountain in Georgia, designed and supervised the carving of Mount Rushmore. He died before the monument was completed, so his son finished the project. (Show the final illustration on page 47.)

Curriculum Connection

Use this book in conjunction with a unit that deals with feats of engineering such as the building of the pyramids of Egypt and the construction of hydroelectric dams, tunnels, bridges, and skyscrapers. Extend the book by having students research and report on careers in different fields of engineering.

Related Books

Similar books by Lynn Curlee are *Liberty* and *Brooklyn Bridge* that tell of the building of the Statue of Liberty and the Brooklyn Bridge. *Those Building Men* by Angela Johnson features the men who labored to build bridges, railroads, skyscrapers, and monuments.

Fun Facts

Bridwell, Norman. **Clifford's Big Book of Things to Know: A Book of Fun Facts**. New York: Scholastic Press, 1999. Unpaged. $10.95. ISBN 0-590-00385-2.

   ■ **PICTURE BOOK—Nonfiction**
   ■ **ALL AGES**

Summary

Using a two-page spread with cartoon-like illustrations, this book provides information about topics such as the body, sports, gardening, pets, space, rocks, and others.

Booktalk/Bookwalk

(Begin by showing the book. Tell children that Clifford and Emily Elizabeth are very curious.) What is it that you are curious about— your body, sports, a garden, pets, space, the seashore—or something else? Clifford and Emily Elizabeth are curious too, and they will tell you about all that and much more!

Curriculum Connections

Children are likely to enjoy studying and researching a topic such as insects and spiders, the seashore, or animal homes using this book as a reference.

Gardens and Gardening

Bogacki, Tomek. **My First Garden**. New York: Frances Foster Books, 2000. Unpaged. $16.00. ISBN 0-374-32518-9.

- ■ **PICTURE BOOK—Fiction**
- ■ **AGES 5–10**

Summary

A man remembers his boyhood, the house and nearby streets, his childhood games, the bicycle he rode to school and to the grassy meadow filled with wildflowers, and the garden that he planted. Delicate illustrations retell the story along with the text.

Booktalk/Bookwalk

Tell the children that they are about to see all of the things, especially the garden, that a man remembers from his childhood. Show the book, turn the pages, and retell the story from the illustrations. Ask, what do you think you'll remember from this year? Last year?

Curriculum Connections

Use this book in conjunction with a gardening activity, either indoors or out. The activity may be as simple as planting bean seeds in Styrofoam cups or as committing as preparing the soil for an outdoor garden plot. Talk about the experience of gardening, experiences that the children may have gardening with family members, and gardening stories that they may have heard from family members. Encourage children to ask family members to tell about their gardening memories. Then have children share those memories with the group.

Spalding, Andrea, and Janet Wilson. **Me and Mr. Mah**. Custer, WA: Orca, 2000. Unpaged. $14.95. ISBN 1-55143-168-8.

- ■ **PICTURE BOOK—Fiction**
- ■ **AGES 4–8**

Summary

When Ian and his mother move to the city, Ian misses his dad and the farm. As he crouches by the fence at the back of the yard plowing a row with his toy tractor, Ian can see a Chinese man tending his garden. Ian and Mr. Mah become friends, tend their gardens, and share their stories and even their special memory boxes.

Booktalk

What is Mr. Mah's memory box doing in the secondhand store? Mr. Mah was my best friend. He lived next door the summer that Mom and I moved from the farm. He gave me sunflower seeds to plant. Then he invited me to visit his garden. His garden was a jungle. He let me touch and sniff. Then he served me tea and told me stories about China. I told him stories about wheat farming on the prairie. Mr. Mah took me to Chinatown and showed me his special box, his memory box. I told him about my dad and I made a memory box. I put my tractor and the postcards from my dad in it. Then Mom and I moved to a little house near my new school. When I found Mr. Mah's memory box in the secondhand store, I knew that something terrible had happened. What could it be? How could I find out?

Curriculum Connections

Have the children plant sunflower seeds either in an outdoor garden or in pots. Talk about how the seeds must change in order to become plants with flowers and more seeds. Ask children how other plants and animals change. Elaborate on the process of change (e.g., the seed puts out roots, then sprouts and shoots, and feeds the roots, sprouts, and shoots until the seed is no more). Encourage students to talk about change in their own lives, then create and share memory boxes. Students can use shoe boxes and decorate them as Ian did to make a memory box.

Seasons

Rucki, Ani. **When the Earth Wakes**. New York: Scholastic Press, 1998. Unpaged. $15.95. ISBN 0-590-05951-3.

- **PICTURE BOOK—Concept Book**
- **AGES 5–8**

Summary

Bold, colorful, stylized illustrations that correspond closely to the simple text take the reader through the seasons of the year with the bear who wakens in early spring, frolics into summer, gets ready for winter during the autumn, and goes back to sleep for the winter.

Bookwalk/Read-Aloud

Turn the pages, point to the pictures, and read the simple text about the bear and the changing seasons of the year.

Curriculum Connections

Read aloud when introducing children to the seasons of the year. Follow up by talking about the seasons. Illustrations lend themselves to charcoal and pastel drawings. Have children draw pictures of the seasons using charcoal and pastels.

Tafuri, Nancy. **Snowy Flowy Blowy**. New York: Scholastic Press, 1999. Unpaged. $15.95. ISBN 0-590-18973-5.

- **PICTURE BOOK—Concept Book**
- **AGES 3–6**

Summary

This gentle book based on an eighteenth-century poem features one word per illustrated page to depict the months of the year. Watercolors celebrate the natural environment with pictures of deer, ducks, a robin and swans, a hummingbird and bluebirds, an egret and sheep, blackbirds, finch, geese, and a cat. Each two-page spread features children playing in the background.

Bookwalk/Read-Aloud

With gentle illustrations and only one word per page, this is a book to show and read aloud.

Curriculum Connections

After showing and reading this book, talk about the months of the year, the changes in the weather, wildlife, and the natural environment. Encourage the children to select a month and draw their own pictures. Use this book for repeated readings and encourage children to chime in to read the one word per page. Then encourage them to substitute other words to describe each month.

Related Books

Other books by Nancy Tafuri are *Will You Be My Friend?*, *Have You Seen My Duckling?*, *I Love You, Little One*, and *Counting to Christmas*.

Senses

Cole, Joanna, and Bruce Degen. **The Magic School Bus Explores the Senses**. New York: Scholastic Press, 1999. 48p. $15.95. ISBN 0-590-44697-5.

- ■ **PICTURE BOOK**
- ■ **AGES 3–10**

Summary

Mr. Wilde, the new assistant principal, takes the children on the magic school bus for a wild ride through the eye, ear, nose, mouth, skin, and brain. Cartoon-like illustrations supplement the text that is enhanced with sidebars, dialogue balloons, charts, and diagrams.

Booktalk

Mr. Wilde, the new assistant principal, climbed into the magic school bus to chase after Ms. Frizzle, and all of the children joined him. Before the children could say, "Don't touch that switch!" Mr. Wilde reached toward the dashboard and another adventure began. This time Ms. Frizzle's cat comes to the rescue.

Curriculum Connections

Use this book as an introduction to studying the senses. Some questions developed in this book are: Why do we need our senses? Which senses are most important? What happens in the brain when we use our senses? The book addresses questions about touch, sight, hearing, taste, and smell. Children may wish to research additional information to add to what is in the book or pose new questions of their own.

Space

Cohn, Arlen. **Solar System SOS**. Denver: Accord, 1998. Unpaged. Illustrated by Don Sullivan. $15.95. ISBN 0-939-25198-1.

■ **PICTURE BOOK**
■ **AGES 3 and up**

Summary

Rotating eyeballs peer through two holes on each page of this colorful fantasy written in rhyme. The problem is that the solar system is totally disrupted when a distant planet borrows the sun. The inside back cover of the book shows the planets, their positions relative to the sun and each other, plus a brief description of each.

Booktalk

When citizens from a far distant planet use their Pull 'n' Push Beam to borrow the sun, temperatures soar on Pluto, plummet on Mercury, and create havoc on the other planets. How can they share the sun without disrupting the solar system?

Curriculum Connections

Although the publisher recommends this book for ages 3 and up, it is more effective with ages 6 and up. Children who know something about the planets will better appreciate the humor and the dilemma.

This book is appropriate for use with a unit about the solar system. It can launch creative speculation, discussion, and writing about "What would happen if _____?" For immediate follow-up, construct a model of the solar system based on the picture of the planets and the brief descriptions of each inside the back cover.

Related Books

Starry Messenger: Galileo Galilei tells the story of Galileo, the scientist, mathematician, astronomer, philosopher, and physicist who determined that the Earth and the planets revolve around the sun. It is reviewed in this section.

Sis, Peter. **Starry Messenger: Galileo Galilei**. New York: Farrar, Straus & Giroux, 2000. Unpaged. $15.95. ISBN 0-374-47027-8.

- **PICTURE BOOK—Nonfiction**
- **AGES 7–12**

Summary

This Caldecott Honor Book (now available in paperback) tells the story of Galileo, the scientist, mathematician, astronomer, philosopher, and physicist who established that Earth was not the center of the universe. A wealth of information and ideas are presented in the readable text, rich illustrations, sidebars, and running time line that begins on the first page and continues to the end of the book.

Booktalk

They said he was born with stars in his eyes. But the stars left his eyes when he was brought to trial. Today we have no question that Earth and the planets revolve around the sun. We have even sent spaceships to explore our solar system. But once upon a time people believed that Earth was the center of the universe. Here is the story of Galileo, the scientist, mathematician, astronomer, philosopher, and physicist who, night after night, studied the sky, wrote down his observations, made maps of what he saw, and literally changed our view of the universe.

Curriculum Connections

The richness of this book requires multiple readings to absorb all of the ideas, then additional readings to integrate the information. Read the simple text aloud. Revisit the book by retelling the story using the illustrations. Have children reconstruct the time line that runs throughout the book. Be sure to include in the time line the birth of Shakespeare, the death of Michelangelo, significant events of Galileo's life, and the laws of the pendulum, falling objects, and floating objects, all of which are in the book. Have children retell the story using the time line. Read and discuss the sidebars.

Demonstrate the law of the pendulum, the law of falling objects, and the law of floating objects. Visit a planetarium or encourage children to view the night sky using a telescope. Extend the book by having children research the lives and beliefs of Ptolemy and Copernicus. Finally, have each child select an aspect of the book that particularly appeals to him or her and respond to that event by talking about it, drawing a picture, writing a poem, or presenting a creative response of his or her own choosing.

Related Books

Galileo's Treasure Box by Catherine Brighton tells the story of Galileo's daughter, Virginia, who slips into his study and opens the small box holding four pieces of glass and a feather.

CHAPTER 3

Social Studies

INTRODUCTION

The burgeoning number of historical fiction titles, stories about contemporary life, and biographies is reflected in the selections included in this chapter. In particular, twentieth-century life and personalities are a recurring theme in books for young readers, especially life during the early 1900s and stories of World War II. Books that address geography and character education are also included in Chapter 3.

AMERICAN HISTORY

Bial, Raymond. **One-Room School**. Boston: Houghton Mifflin, 1999. 48p. $15.00. ISBN 0-395-90514-1.

- ■ **PICTURE BOOK**
- ■ **AGES 9–14**

Summary

This book chronicles the history of the one-room schoolhouse across America from the 1700s to the 1950s. Colored photographs enhance the informative, expository text.

Booktalk

Can you imagine walking miles through woods or open fields, in sun, wind, rain, or snow, carrying your lunch pail and books on your way to school? What do you suppose your school would be like once you got there? (Show picture.) Here it is—only one room with a potbellied stove in the center or corner, a bucket of water with a dipper by the door, coat hooks across the back wall, and hard benches to sit on. Young children and older children are all together with only one teacher. What games did the children play at recess? How did the children learn? What happened to these schoolhouses?

Curriculum Connections

Research the history of the one-room school in your community. Are there any local one-room buildings still standing and in use as schools or museums? Can you find desks and even books that were used in the one-room school? Are there senior citizens in your community who attended or remember the one-room school? What stories do they have to tell?

Brooks, Nigel, and Abigail Horner. **Town Mouse House: How We Lived One Hundred Years Ago**. New York: Walker, 2000. 32p. $15.95. ISBN 0-8027-8732-0.

- ■ **PICTURE BOOK**
- ■ **AGES 5–8**

Summary

Augustus John Town Mouse introduces us to his family, shows us around his house, and tells us how his family lived in 1900. Cartoon-like illustrations supplement the humorous narrative text.

Booktalk

Augustus John Town Mouse has invited you to step back to the year 1900 and to visit his house and family, not in the country but in the town. Augustus John Town Mouse lives with his Mama and Papa and his sister and brother. His family has servants: a butler, a cook, a nanny, and a parlor maid. They even have a governess who comes to the house every morning to teach the school lessons to Augustus John and his sister Kate. Augustus John's Mama has a seamstress who comes to the house for fittings so she can make their clothes. Augustus John has promised to show you his family's clothes and the toys that he and his brother and sister play with, and take you into Papa's study and to the town square. Want to go?

Curriculum Connections

Have the children invite Augustus John Town Mouse into their homes to meet their families, show him their clothes and toys, take him to school, and show him their town—the shopping center, mall, parks, and places of interest. Have them invite Augustus John to stay for dinner and to spend the night. Brainstorm and on a semantic chart (see Appendix A) record what children will show Augustus John. Then have them draw pictures and write a book about life today in their homes and community.

Related Books

Country Mouse Cottage: How We Lived One Hundred Years Ago depicts country life in 1900.

Colman, Penny. **Girls: A History of Growing Up Female in America**. New York: Scholastic Press, 2000. 192p. $18.95. ISBN 0-590-37129-0.

- **CHAPTER BOOK—Nonfiction**
- **AGES 10 and up**

Summary

Ten chapters with drawings, photographs, and maps address aspects of being a girl in America from the first Ice Age (with people who probably traveled across the Bering Sea land bridge), to the early colonies, then to the nineteenth century, the early 1900s, and finally to today. The book begins with an "Author's Note" and ends with "Selected Sources for Further Reading." Although this book may be of greater interest to girls than to boys, boys may be interested in learning more about the experiences of their mothers and grandmothers.

Booktalk

What do you suppose it was like to grow up in America 100 or even 200 years ago? Would you wear the clothes, play the games, and go to school as you do today? Come, meet the girls who crossed the land bridge over the Bering Sea, who crossed the ocean to the New World, and who crossed the continent by wagons and oxcarts. Read about the kinds of lives your ancestors had when they were young girls.

Curriculum Connections

Make a time line showing how the lives of girls changed over the years. Ask your grandmothers, great-grandmothers, and senior citizens what their lives were like when they were children.

Related Books

Other books that address being a girl in America and that are reviewed in the Social Studies chapter of this book are: *Mary Geddy's Day: A Colonial Girl in Williamsburg*, *Molly Bannaky*, *The Promise Quilt*, and *You Forgot Your Skirt Amelia Bloomer!*

Garland, Sherry. **Voices of the Alamo.** New York: Scholastic Press, 2000. Unpaged. Illustrated by Ronald Himler. $16.95. ISBN 0-590-98833-6.

■ **PICTURE BOOK—Mexico**
■ **AGES 9–12**

Summary

The history of the Alamo is retold through first-person narratives by people who lived there. The stories begin with a Payaya Indian girl in 1500. They continue with a conquistador in 1542, a padre in 1745, a Spanish soldier in 1803, a Tejano rancher in 1821, a Texan farmer in 1830, and major players in the conflict with Mexico that culminated in the battle of the Alamo with General Sam Houston in 1836. The stories end with Clara Driscoll who in 1904 was instrumental in buying the old mission and preserving it as a historic landmark. The book concludes with a two-page expository history of the Alamo.

Booktalk

Have you heard of the Alamo? Do you know the story? Not just about the battles, but the *whole* story, starting in the 1500s? Come listen. The story starts with a Payaya maiden who is gathering pecans beside the river. Then comes a Spanish conquistador riding his horse in search of gold. A bare-footed padre comes next to build a mission along the river. After that soldiers come to the Alamo. Listen! Who else is coming? Santa Anna, Davy Crockett, and Sam Houston are only a few more who will tell you their stories and the story of the Alamo.

Curriculum Connections

Use the book to reconstruct a time line. (See Appendix A.) Assign each child a character. Have the children practice and read aloud the lines of their characters.

Giblin, James Cross. **The Century That Was**. New York: Atheneum Books for Young Readers, 2000. 164p. $19.95. ISBN 0-689-82281-2.

- **CHAPTER BOOK—Nonfiction**
- **AGES 10 and up**

Summary

Authors such as Eve Bunting, Walter Dean Myers, Lois Lowry, Milton Meltzer, Katherine Paterson, and others wrote essays about life in the United States from 1901 to 2000. They wrote about topics such as immigrants, World War I, inventions, women's rights, civil rights, fashions, politics, religion, and more.

Booktalk

Do you have a favorite author? Or perhaps there's a topic that you're really interested in such as sports, fashions, inventions, women's rights, or World War I? Favorite authors Eve Bunting, Lois Lowry, Walter Dean Myers, and others write about these topics and more in *The Century That Was*.

Curriculum Connections

This book could be used to organize and motivate additional reading and research about the topics addressed. Ten chapters address ten different topics such as immigrants, World War I, women's rights, and civil rights. Recommendations for Further Reading are listed in the back of the book. Group students and have them read and report on topics of interest.

Related Books

Books that address some of the topics written about in *The Century That Was* and are reviewed in the Social Studies chapter of this book are: *Town Mouse House: How We Lived One Hundred Years Ago*, *My Name Is Not Gussie*, *The Memory Coat*, and *Amelia and Eleanor Go for a Ride*.

McKissack, Patricia, and Fredrick L. McKissack. **Black Hands, White Sails: The Story of African-American Whalers**. New York: Scholastic Press, 1999. 147p. $15.95. ISBN 0-590-48313-7.

- **CHAPTER BOOK—African Americans**
- **AGES 10 and up**

Summary

This book tells the story of the African Americans who served on the whaling ships of the nineteenth century. Although serving on a whaling ship was a hard life, it was also a life by which African Americans might acquire a measure of wealth and power. This is an authentic account of nineteenth-century racial diversity as well as whales and whaling. Frederick Douglass is a noted African American who served on a whaling ship. A time line at the end of the book that recounts important dates from 1441 to 1917 and a bibliography provide additional information.

Booktalk

Some of the first slaves served on whaling vessels, beginning in 1716 through the Golden Age of Whaling, which lasted from 1815 to 1865. These African Americans founded whaling families, established schools for their children, and organized their own churches including the African Methodist Episcopal Church. Freed African Americans spearheaded the purchase and settlement of the West African country of Liberia. Others such as Frederick Douglass served as whaling hands then returned to the land to live as freedmen. Read about the African Americans who acquired a measure of wealth and power by serving on the whaling ships of the nineteenth century.

Curriculum Connections

Use this book in conjunction with a unit on African American history. Form eight groups of children. Assign one chapter to each group. Have each group read the assigned chapter, identify and research additional information about individuals such as Crispus Attucks and Frederick Douglass in each chapter, and prepare an oral presentation about the chapter and its people. This book could also prompt inquiry into the history of the whaling business.

Related Books

Good-bye for Today: The Diary of a Young Girl at Sea is the story of Laura, who sailed to the Arctic aboard her father's whaling ship. It is a fictional account based on the true journal and experiences of two young girls who sailed aboard their fathers' whaling ships.

Priceman, Marjorie. **My Nine Lives by Clio**. New York: Atheneum, 1998. Unpaged. $16.00. ISBN 0-689-811-357.

■ **PICTURE BOOK**
■ **AGES 5–8**

Summary

The "Publisher's Note" explains that not only is this book based on the journal of Clio, the cat who lived nine lives in nine different historical times, it is also written in Clio's own words and uses her own illustrations.

Booktalk

I'm Clio the cat. I've lived nine fascinating lives in which I've changed the course of history with my creativity, adventures, and inventions. I am also a very talented author and illustrator. In fact, I have recorded and illustrated this journal of the stories of my nine lives, beginning with my first life in 3000 B.C. in Mesopotamia. What do you think it would be like to live in another time? Come with me to journey through time and place. Discover everything I have contributed to your life and your world. You might be surprised.

Curriculum Connections

Present the book and turn the pages to show the pictures as you tell about Clio's lives and accomplishments. The content and format of this book are likely to appeal to readers of all ages. Clio's journal might serve as a model for sequencing and retelling history or social studies events. Some teachers might want to encourage students to change the style of Clio's writing from a journal to letters, poems, or fairy tales. For immediate follow-up, create a time line of Clio's accomplishments. (See Appendix A.) Encourage students to revisit the book in order to create the time line.

Ryan, Pam Munoz. **Amelia and Eleanor Go for a Ride**. New York: Scholastic Press, 1999. Unpaged. Illustrated by Brian Selznick. $16.95. ISBN 0-590-96075-X.

- **PICTURE BOOK**
- **AGES 5–9**

Summary

This book is based on a true account of Amelia Earhart and Eleanor Roosevelt, who were good friends. During a dinner at the White House on an evening in April 1933, the two excused themselves, flew to Baltimore, Maryland, and back with Amelia Earhart as pilot, took a ride in Eleanor

Roosevelt's car with Eleanor as driver, then returned to the White House for dessert. The dessert recipe is included at the back of the book.

Booktalk

What would you think if your mother invited friends for dinner, then in the middle of dinner left with her friend to fly to a neighboring city? That is exactly what Eleanor Roosevelt, first lady of the United States, did the night she invited her friend Amelia Earhart, the first woman pilot to fly solo across the Atlantic Ocean, to dinner at the White House. Dressed in their high heels, evening gowns, and long white gloves the two women, over the protests of the Secret Service men, left in the middle of dinner. Where do you think they went? What did they do? Would they make it back in time for dessert?

Curriculum Connections

This story is written in such a way that it compares and contrasts the two main characters. Either read aloud or have the children silently read the book, and then discuss the characters of Eleanor and Amelia. Have the children complete a Venn diagram (see Appendix A) that compares and contrasts the two women. Have the children learn more about the two women who were friends. Consider showing the PBS video *Amelia Earhart* (produced by Nancy Porter, 1993, approximately one hour), which tells the story of her record-breaking flights, aerial exhibitions, promotional commitments, and finally her disappearance with her plane in 1937. (Be sure to preview the hour-long video. You may wish to select episodes to share with the children.) Another PBS video *Eleanor Roosevelt* (produced by Ambrica Productions Inc., 1999, approximately two and a half hours) tells the story of Eleanor's life. (Because it is two-and-a-half hours long, you may wish to select episodes to share with the children.) Finally, serve angel food cake with strawberries and whipped cream as a treat. This is the dessert served at the White House the night Eleanor and Amelia went for a ride. The recipe is included at the back of the book.

Waters, Kate. **Mary Geddy's Day: A Colonial Girl in Williamsburg**. New York: Scholastic Press, 1999. 40p. Photographs by Russ Kendall. $16.95. ISBN 0-590-92925-9.

■ **PICTURE BOOK**
■ **AGES 7–12**

Summary

Nine-year-old Emily Smith portrays Mary Geddy, whose father was a silversmith in Williamsburg. Text and colored photographs reenact a day in Williamsburg—a special day—the day the Fifth Virginia Convention voted for independence from Great Britain. The book ends with "Notes About Williamsburg in Colonial Times," "The Prelude to Independence," "Slavery in the Virginia Colony," "Native Americans in Colonial Virginia," "The Geddy Family," "Girlhood in Eighteenth-Century Williamsburg," and recipes for "Making Sweet Bags for Linen from Lavender and Apple Pie."

Bookwalk

Present the book, turn the pages, and show the photographs that tell the story of a day in colonial Williamsburg, Virginia, as experienced by ten-year-old Mary Geddy. Begin on page 4 with the photograph of Mary. Pages 6–7 show Mary waking up, washing, and getting dressed. Pages 8–9 show Christopher, the houseboy, carrying out the chamber pot, Mary and her sister, Elizabeth, going downstairs, the Geddy house, and townspeople in the street. Pages 10–11 show Mary at the market carrying coins for eggs, and visiting with her friend, Anne. Pages 12–13 show delegates arguing with one another, and Mary's family sitting down to breakfast. Pages 14–15 show Mary with her family engaged in moving the table and chairs after breakfast, sewing, and learning letters. On pages 16–17 Mama and family members are baking a pie. On the next four pages we see Mary and Elizabeth in the garden. Then on pages 22–23 Mary goes to her father's silver shop to call her father and brothers for dinner. We see the family at dinner. After dinner Mama sends Mary and her brother to the store to get a treat for their sister. On pages 24–25 we see the music teacher giving Mary a spinet lesson. When the family hears a commotion and gunfire, they run up the stairs to the balcony where they can see what is happening in the street. The colonies have declared their independence from England! On the next four pages Mary, her family, and townspeople walk down the street and gather at the capitol. On pages 30–31 they pass a man taking down the sign at the King's Arms Tavern as they return home for their supper. After supper, Anne reads *Aesop's Fables* to her brother and sister. On their way to bed they greet Papa's guests in the parlor. Finally, Mary watches the town bonfire from the upstairs balcony on pages 32–33, and then goes to bed on page 34.

Curriculum Connections

Learn more about Mary, her family, and life in colonial Williamsburg by visiting the Web site at http://ColonialWilliamsburg .net/history. The Geddy house and family are featured as well as details about daily life in colonial Williamsburg. Extend the activity by using information from the book and the Web site to put together a newspaper that includes news, a society page, editorials, a classified section, and advertisements that reflect daily life in colonial Williamsburg.

Related Books

To learn more about girls' daily lives in the eighteenth century see *Girls: A History of Growing Up Female in America*, which is reviewed in this section.

Yue, Charlotte, and David Yue. **The Wigwam and the Long-house.** Boston: Houghton Mifflin, 2000. 118p. $15.00. ISBN 0-395-84169-0.

■ **CHAPTER BOOK—Native Americans**
■ **AGES 8–12**

Summary

The Yues give an account of the life of the woodland Indians from the Atlantic Ocean west to the Mississippi River Valley and from Canada south to Virginia and North Carolina. They describe the people and their tribes and confederations, their use of the land, how they built their homes and lived together, their culture, how they traveled, what happened with the arrival of Europeans, and finally their lives today.

Booktalk

Who lived here in America first? The Iroquoians and the Algonquians, who lived in the eastern woodlands before the arrival of Europeans, shared common bloodlines and language stocks. What kind of homes did they have? How did they survive? What happened to them when the Europeans came?

Curriculum Connections

Divide the children into two groups. Assign one group to the wigwam, the other group to the longhouse (a communal dwelling). Have each group prepare a story with drawings about who they are, how the wigwam or longhouse is built, and what it is like to live in a wigwam or longhouse. Have each group share their story and drawings with the other group.

Then have one group prepare a story with drawings about community life. Have the other group prepare a story with drawings about the political organization of the woodland people, other structures that they built, and their means of travel. Have each group share their story and drawings with the other group.

AUTOBIOGRAPHIES AND BIOGRAPHIES

Brown, Don. **Rare Treasure: Mary Anning and Her Remarkable Discoveries**. Boston: Houghton Mifflin, 1999. Unpaged. $15.00. ISBN 0-395-92286-0.

- ■ **PICTURE BOOK—Nonfiction**
- ■ **AGES 7–12**

Summary

Pen and ink and watercolors illustrate this nontraditional (intended for fluent rather than beginning readers) picture book that tells the story of Mary Anning, the first commercial fossil collector. She lived from 1799 to 1845 and unearthed fossils along England's shore. The pterodactyl that she discovered is still displayed at the British Natural History Museum. Children are likely to be fascinated by the girl who dug up dinosaurs.

Booktalk

They said that it was the lightning. Mary was just a baby when lightning struck the tree. Mary's nursemaid and two other young women died. Mary survived and grew up to be a very special person.

Mary Anning was poor but curious and bright. She lived near the sea in the 1800s. Mary visited the rocky beaches with her brothers and her father who taught them how to look for fossils. Have you ever looked for fossils? Have you ever found any? Well, Mary did! She found an ichthyosaur, a plesiosaur, and even the pterodactyl that is still on display at the British Natural History Museum.

Curriculum Connections

This book would be appropriate to use in conjunction with a unit on dinosaurs or careers. Have students gather, identify, classify, and display specimens from the natural environment.

Related Books

The Fossil Girl: Mary Anning's Dinosaur Discovery by Catherine Brighton is another account of Mary Anning.

Corey, Shana. **You Forgot Your Skirt Amelia Bloomer!** New York: Scholastic Press, 2000. Unpaged. Illustrated by Chesley McLaren. $16.95. ISBN 0-439-07819-9.

■ **PICTURE BOOK—Humorous Account**
■ **AGES 5–8**

Summary

Lively, cartoon-like illustrations supplement this humorous account of rebellious Amelia Bloomer who scandalized the townspeople of Seneca Falls, New York, by designing and wearing pantaloons under her shortened skirt. Because she wanted women everywhere to know about the new clothes, she wrote about them in her own newspaper. Woman quickly replied, asking where or how they could get or make the new fashion. The "Author's Note" gives a short biography of Amelia Bloomer, an early leader of the women's rights movement.

Booktalk

Girls and women haven't always worn blue jeans. About 150 years ago, they wore corsets so tight that they could hardly breathe and skirts so long and full that they got stuck in doorways. Little girls couldn't run, jump, or play because the clothes they wore didn't allow it. But Amelia Bloomer changed all of that. She designed and wore pantaloons under her shortened skirt. The townspeople were shocked when they saw her on the street in her new clothes. What do you suppose they said?

Curriculum Connections

Although the book is intended for readers five to eight years of age, the content would also be of interest to older readers. Engage children in a discussion of fashions and how they have changed. Begin by talking about the kinds of clothing women wear today. Then talk about the clothing that women wore 50 and 100 years ago. How have women's fashions changed? How have men's fashions changed? What kind of clothing is comfortable to wear and easy to move in? What kind of clothing is uncomfortable and restricts movement? Have young children draw a picture of comfortable clothing and a picture of uncomfortable clothing. Have older children research how fashions changed over time.

Discuss women's rights and how women's lives have changed (e.g., the right to vote, to own property, and to earn equal pay). Have older children research other leaders of the women's rights movement such as Elizabeth Cady Stanton who is mentioned in the book.

Giblin, James Cross. **The Amazing Life of Benjamin Franklin**. New York: Scholastic Press, 2000. 48p. Illustrated by Michael Dooling. $17.95. ISBN 0-590-48354-2.

■ **PICTURE BOOK—Nonfiction**
■ **AGES 8–12**

Summary

This is a picture book biography of Benjamin Franklin from birth to death. It concludes with a list of important dates from his life, a description of a few of his inventions, and selected sayings from *Poor Richard's Almanac*.

Booktalk

He was a printer, an inventor, a writer, and a statesman. He was one of seventeen children and at the age of ten went to work in his father's candle- and soap-making shop. Because he loved to read and was good at spelling, his father arranged for him to work as an apprentice in his brother's print shop. It was there that he began writing. Years later he started a weekly newspaper and wrote *Poor Richard's Almanac*, which included a calendar, weather forecasts, poems, and sayings. Who was he? (Let the children guess, then hold up the book and tell them.)

Curriculum Connections

Have students research to learn more about Ben Franklin's inventions and *Poor Richard's Almanac*. Use the time line in the back of the book as a guide to developing a chronological retelling of his life. For example, have one child begin as Ben Franklin the boy growing up in a family of seventeen children and working in his father's shop. Then have a second child continue as the young man apprenticed to his brother. Have a third child continue with the next significant event in Ben Franklin's life and so on until his death.

Gold, Alison Leslie. **A Special Fate Chiune Sugihara: Hero of the Holocaust**. New York: Scholastic Press, 2000. 160p. $15.95. ISBN 0-590-39525-4.

- **CHAPTER BOOK—World War II; Japan; Jews**
- **AGES 10 and up**

Summary

Chiune Sugihara was a Japanese diplomat who served as vice consul in Lithuania. Against orders from his government, he issued more than 2,193 transit visas that allowed Jewish refugees from Germany and Poland to travel through Russia and Japan where they could board ships to places such as Curacao and Shanghai.

Booktalk

The refugees kept coming. They were Lithuanian Jews who wanted transit visas to flee the approaching German army. Chiune anguished over their suffering, their need for help, and the risks to himself and his own family. The Japanese government had denied this request to issue the visas. What was he to do? What would be the consequences of his actions to the refugees, to himself, and to his own family?

Curriculum Connections

Using a world map, find the countries that figure prominently in this book (i.e., Japan, Russia, Lithuania, Poland, and Germany). Find the cities of Curacao and Shanghai. Trace the routes that people traveled. Have students read and retell the experiences of Chiune and his family and the experiences of the Jewish families such as Zelda and Masha

Bernstein, the Ganors, and Zorach Warhaftig. If you can find someone who escaped from Europe before or during World War II, invite him or her to meet with your group and share the stories of people who helped them.

Jimenez, Francisco. **The Circuit: Stories from the Life of a Migrant Child.** Boston: Houghton Mifflin, 1999. 128p. $15.00. ISBN 0-395-97902-1.

- ■ **CHAPTER BOOK—Autobiography; Mexican Americans; ESOL**
- ■ **AGES 11 and up**

Summary

The author writes of his experiences as a migrant child. Each of the twelve chapters is a self-contained story or episode; however, the chapters flow one into the other. Chapters can be read in isolation, in or out of sequence. In the "Author's Note" at the end of the book the author tells more about himself as a writer and his experiences growing up.

Booktalk

My name is Francisco Jimenez. I'd like to tell you something about myself, about what it was like to grow up as a Mexican American migrant child. When I was very young, I lived with my family near Guadalajara, Mexico. Papa talked about going to California where life would be better and he could earn good money. Finally, the day came when we took the train to California, leaving friends and neighbors behind.

We lived in labor camps; picked strawberries, cotton, and grapes; moved with the seasons; and sometimes went to school. I got headaches in school from listening so hard to the teacher talk. I don't know what she said, because she talked in English and I speak Spanish. If I let my mind wander, my head didn't hurt. When the teacher read stories from books with pictures, I made up my own stories. Now I want to share my stories with you.

Curriculum Connections

Use this book as a model for writing about personal or family experiences. Children who are English speakers of other languages may be encouraged to talk and write of their experiences.

Related Books

Francisco Jimenez developed the first story from this book into a nontraditional (intended for fluent rather than beginning readers) picture book titled *La Mariposa*.

Linnea, Sharon. **Princess Ka'iulani: Hope of a Nation, Heart of a People**. Grand Rapids, MI: Eerdmans Books for Young Readers, 1999. 234p. $18.00. ISBN 0-8028-5145-2.

- ■ **CHAPTER BOOK—Hawaiians**
- ■ **AGES 10 and up**

Summary

The biography of Hawaii's last princess and the story of the last of Hawaii's monarchy is also the story of the U.S. annexation of Hawaii. Princess Ka'iulani, daughter of a Hawaiian princess and a Scottish businessman, was born in 1876 and was raised to become the Queen of Hawaii. Beautiful, intelligent, graceful, and witty, Princess Ka'iulani was educated in England and Europe and prepared by Hawaiian royalty to rule their country. At the same time, political forces were moving to destroy the Hawaiian monarchy and to annex Hawaii to the United States. Instead of ruling, Princess Ka'iulani represented her country in the United States and unsuccessfully fought against annexation. She died at the age of twenty-two within months of annexation. Black-and-white photographs supplement the readable text.

Booktalk

"Uneducated savages!" That's what American newspapers wrote about Hawaiians. When Princess Ka'iulani arrived in New York from London, reporters gathered to meet the "barbarian princess." Instead they met a beautiful, intelligent, fashionable, and educated young woman who spoke with grace and eloquence.

King Kalakaua knew that the future queen and ruler of Hawaii must hold her own against well-educated foreign rulers; therefore, thirteen-year-old Princess Ka'iulani was sent to England for schooling. But while the princess attended school in England, political forces were building toward the overthrow of the Hawaiian monarchy and the annexation of Hawaii by the United States. Princess Ka'iulani was only seventeen years old, but she was determined to persuade the American people, the Congress, and the president to support continued independence for Hawaii.

Read about the "hope of a nation, heart of a people" who charmed the Americans and endeared herself to her own people!

Curriculum Connections

Include in a social studies unit about Hawaii. Create a time line that shows the history of Hawaii and its annexation to the United States.

Related Books

Kaiiulani: The People's Princess by Ellen Emerson White is one of The Royal Diaries Series.

McGill, Alice. **Molly Bannaky**. Boston: Houghton Mifflin, 1999. Unpaged. Illustrated by Chris K. Soentpiet. $16.00. ISBN 0-395-72287-0.

■ **PICTURE BOOK—Nonfiction; Diversity; African Americans**
■ **AGES 4–8**

Summary

Molly Bannaky is an orphaned English milkmaid sentenced to seven years of bondage in the New World for spilling the farmer's milk. After serving her seven years of indentured servitude, Mary stakes a claim and buys an African slave whom she eventually frees and marries. Their grandson, Benjamin Banneker, becomes a scientist and mathematician who makes numerous contributions to his field. The book ends with a historical note that elaborates on the times.

Booktalk

She might have been hanged, but because she could read, Molly's life was spared. Instead of being sentenced to death by hanging for spilling the farmer's milk, Molly, an orphaned English milkmaid, was sentenced to seven years of bondage in the New World. Molly worked for a planter for seven years, then single-handedly staked her claim in the wilderness, and bought a slave. But that's only the beginning of Mary's amazing life. Find out what happened to the slave and how Molly managed in the face of tremendous adversity. One of her grandchildren became a famous scientist and mathematician. Do you know who he was?

Curriculum Connections

Have the children research indentured servants and prepare a report. Encourage students to find out more about Molly's grandson and to learn more about their own families' heritage by interviewing parents, grandparents, aunts, or uncles.

Myers, W. D. At Her Majesty's Request: An African Princess in Victorian England. New York: Scholastic Press, 1999. 146p. $15.95. ISBN 0-590-48669-1.

- **CHAPTER BOOK—Multicultural; Africa**
- **AGES 10 and up**

Summary

Sarah Forbes Benetta is an African princess who is rescued by a British naval officer after raiders attack her village and kidnap her. Sarah is taken to England where she becomes a godchild of Queen Victoria. She lives in London with her rescuer, Commander Forbes, and his family until he dies, after which she returns to Africa. After four years in Africa, Sarah returns to London where she makes extended visits to Windsor castle and becomes close friends with Queen Victoria's daughter, Princess Alice. A month after Princess Alice's wedding, Sarah is also married, but to a man she does not love. With her new husband Sarah returns to Africa where she teaches in a school for African girls. Sarah has three children and finds happiness in her marriage and her life, even though she often has suffered from poor health, until she dies at the age of thirty-eight.

Booktalk

Sarah Forbes Benetta was only two years old when raiders attacked her village in West Africa. Because her face bore the tribal markings of a princess, Sarah was kidnapped by the raiders and then rescued by a British naval officer. Find out what became of this African princess in *At Her Majesty's Request.*

Curriculum Connections

We tend to be unaware of African experiences outside of the United States and to overlook the early experiences of free African

Americans who were not slaves on Southern plantations. Explore the diversity of African and African American experiences using the titles suggested below in "Related Books."

Divide students into three groups with each group reading one book. Have students read and discuss the differing experiences. Then have students in each group become the characters from their book, introduce themselves, and get acquainted with the characters from the other two books.

Related Books

See *Molly Bannaky*, reviewed in this chapter, for the story of Benjamin Banneker's grandmother. *Black Hands, White Sails*, also reviewed in this chapter, tells the story of free African Americans, including Frederick Douglass, who served on nineteenth-century whaling ships.

Rumford, James. **Seeker of Knowledge: The Man Who Deciphered Egyptian Hieroglyphs**. Boston: Houghton Mifflin, 2000. Unpaged. $15.00. ISBN 0-395-97934-X.

- ■ PICTURE BOOK—Nonfiction
- ■ AGES 7–12

Summary

It was a Frenchman, Jean-François Champollion, who was the first to translate the Egyptian hieroglyphics. The story of his work is augmented with sample hieroglyphics interspersed throughout the text. At the very end, a chart shows the Egyptian words written in hieroglyphics, their pronunciations, and English translations.

Booktalk

(Hold up a picture of hieroglyphs.) What do you think this means? How would you find out? Jean-François Champollion was only seven years old when he decided that he would go to Egypt someday. He was eleven years old when he became fascinated with Egyptian hieroglyphics and decided that someday he would learn to read Egyptian writing. Up until then, no one had deciphered the hieroglyphs. For many years Jean-François studied, trying to figure out what letters the Egyptian hieroglyphics represented. Then a friend sent the names of pharaohs copied from a temple wall. Did he crack the code?

Curriculum Connections

Introduce the book by writing the hieroglyphics for "never give up" on a board or flip chart and reading the hieroglyphics in Egyptian. (The hieroglyphics and Egyptian pronunciation are given on the second to the last page of the book.) Retell the story by paging through the book and showing children the hieroglyphics written on each page. Encourage the children to learn more about Egyptian hieroglyphics by using references cited in the book. Have the children research additional sources of information including Web sites.

Related Books

The Shipwrecked Sailor: An Egyptian Tale with Hieroglyphs by Tamara Bower is a story that was found on a papyrus scroll of hieroglyphs dating from the nineteenth century B.C. Phrases from the story appear in hieroglyphs with their literal translations. An explanation about hieroglyphs and their symbols, as well as suggested further readings about hieroglyphs, appear in the back of the book.

Wells, Rosemary. **Mary on Horseback: Three Mountain Stories**. New York: Dial, 1999. 54p. $16.99. ISBN 0-670-88923-7.

- **CHAPTER BOOK—Short Stories**
- **AGES 9–12**

Summary

Rosemary Wells retells three stories told by Mary Breckinridge, founder of the Frontier Nursing Service. The first chapter establishes the time and setting as 1923 in the Appalachian Mountains of Kentucky where medical treatment was close to nonexistent. Mary Breckinridge arrived as a nurse and was determined to build a hospital. The next three chapters tell the stories of John Hawkins and his Pa who nearly lost his leg in a logging accident, of Margaret Ireland a registered nurse from Scotland, and of Pearl whose Mamma died in childbirth. The last chapter is a short biography of Mary Breckinridge.

Booktalk

Step back in time to 1923. Travel into the hills of Kentucky. Meet John Hawkins and his Pa, Margaret Ireland from Scotland, and Pearl. Find out how Mary Breckinridge changed each of their lives.

Curriculum Connections

Use this book in conjunction with a study of real people or a study of life then and now. Have students interview grandparents about their lives, and then write a story based on what they learned.

CONCEPT BOOKS

Atwell, Debby. **River**. Boston: Houghton Mifflin, 1999. 31p. $15.00. ISBN 0-395-93546-6.

- **PICTURE BOOK**
- **AGES 4–8**

Summary

Changes occur over time along the river, which evolves from a pristine wilderness to a congested urban environment. The message of preserving the natural environment is communicated when the congestion is relieved, the river rests, trees grow, and balance is restored.

Booktalk/Bookwalk

(Introduce the book by showing the illustrations and retelling the story.) In the beginning the river was a quiet place where animals came to drink. Then Native Americans made their homes along its shore, followed by European settlers. Towns grew into cities with factories, warehouses, and businesses while steamboats, trains, and automobiles replaced sailing ships and trains. The river became congested and ugly until the people took down factories and warehouses, planted trees, and let the river rest. Balance was restored and people lived in harmony with the river.

Curriculum Connections

(Discuss the following questions.) What animals and plants originally lived in the river? What happened to them? What animals and plants live near the river now? Research the history of your town. Write and illustrate a book that documents the changes in the natural environment that occurred over time.

Related Books

Barn, a similar book by Debby Atwell, is reviewed on the flap of the book cover.

Bang, Molly. **When Sophie Gets Angry—Really, Really Angry . . .** New York: Blue Sky Press, 1999. Unpaged. ISBN 0-590-18979-4.

■ **PICTURE BOOK—Feelings**
■ **AGES 3–7**

Summary

Vibrant, dynamic illustrations supplement the simple text that tells how Sophie runs away, climbs a tree, and finds comfort after she gets very angry.

Booktalk

Have you ever been angry? Sophie has. Now she is really angry with her sister who took her stuffed gorilla away from her. What do you do when you get mad? Sophie kicks, screams, and roars until she's ready to explode. Do you do that? Then Sophie runs away. She runs until she cries. Finally, she climbs into a tree, feels the breeze, and watches the water until she is comforted. When Sophie feels better, she goes home to her family and isn't angry anymore. What makes you feel better when you're angry?

Curriculum Connections

Use this book to explore feelings. Invite children to talk about what they do when they get angry. What are good ways to express anger? What are hurtful ways? Have them draw a picture of what it feels like to be angry.

Chwast, Seymour. **Traffic Jam.** Boston: Houghton Mifflin, 1999. Unpaged. $15.00. ISBN 0-395-97495-X.

■ **PICTURE BOOK—Traffic**
■ **AGES 4–8**

Summary

Traffic Jam is an interactive, foldout book with cartoon-like illustrations. The story line is about a Mama Cat, who held up traffic when she carried her kitten across a busy street.

Read-Aloud

Introduce the book by showing the illustrations and reading aloud. Open the centerfold and engage children in a discussion of the traffic jam.

Curriculum Connections

Ask the children if they have ever been in a traffic jam. What happened? Were cars stopped in the intersection so that cars coming from the other direction could not make turns? Was cross traffic stopped? Did drivers honk? Were pedestrians able to cross the street? What do you suppose people in the traffic jam said? Place sticky notes over the dialogue bubbles in the centerfold. Reread and ask the children to write in their own dialogue.

Geisert, Bonnie, and Arthur Geisert. **Mountain Town**. Boston: Walter Lorraine Books, 2000. 32p. $16.00. ISBN 0-395-95390-1.

- ■ **PICTURE BOOK**
- ■ **AGES 5–10**

Summary

This book takes the reader through a year in a mountain town.

Read-Aloud

Show the illustrations and read aloud.

Curriculum Connections

Detailed illustrations and simple text lend themselves to rereadings and discussions about life in the mountain town. Use this book as a model for writing and illustrating a book that depicts life in your community over a year.

Related Books

The Geiserts have written three similar books: *River Town*, *Prairie Town*, and *Desert Town*.

Joslin, Mary. **The Goodbye Boat**. Grand Rapids, MI: Eerdmans Books for Young Readers, 1999. Unpaged. Illustrated by Claire St Louis Little. $16.00. ISBN 0-8028-5186-X.

■ **PICTURE BOOK—Death**
■ **AGES 5–10**

Summary

Simple text and illustrations gently represent the experience of loss, grief, and renewed life.

Read-Aloud

Create a quiet, reflective environment with soft lighting and soft background music. Read aloud and show the illustrations.

Curriculum Connections

Use this book in conjunction with the exploration of the experiences of death, loss, and grief. This little book offers hope in the midst of loss. It can be used to reflect on the experience of loss and healing.

Yolen, Jane, and Mark Teague. **How Do Dinosaurs Say Good Night?** New York: Blue Sky Press, 2000. Unpaged. $15.95. ISBN 0-590-31681-8.

■ **PICTURE BOOK—Bedtime; ESOL**
■ **AGES 3–7**

Summary

A simple read-aloud, perfect for bedtime, about how dinosaurs give big kisses, turn out the light, tuck in their tails, and whisper "Good Night" rather than throw tantrums at bedtime.

Booktalk

How do you suppose a dinosaur says good night? Does he pout and sulk, have a tantrum, or do naughty things? Does he read a book, sing a song, turn out his light, and shut his eyes? If you were a dinosaur, how would you say good night?

Curriculum Connections

Read aloud and show the pictures. Engage children in a conversation about how they say good night in their homes. Share ways to say good night in other languages such as, *"buenos noches"* (Spanish). Consider using this book with English speakers of other languages (ESOL) students.

HISTORICAL FICTION

Brill, Marlene Targ. **Diary of a Drummer Boy**. Brookfield, CT: Millbrook Press, 1998. 47p. Illustrations by Michael Garland. $23.90. ISBN 0-7613-0118-6.

- **CHAPTER BOOK—The Civil War**
- **AGES 9–12**

Summary

Full-page color illustrations supplement the fictional diary of a young boy who really was a drummer boy during the Civil War. Orion Howe and his brother Lyston were ages twelve and ten, respectively, when they became drummers for the military. The boys served with General William Sherman in the 55th Regiment. Orion was wounded in the battle of Vicksburg, sent home to recuperate, and then reenlisted in the 55th Regiment.

He had the distinction of being the youngest and longest-serving drummer from Illinois in the Civil War. After the war, President Lincoln made it possible for Orion to attend the Naval Academy. He later became a dentist. In 1896, Orion was awarded the Congressional Medal of Honor for bravery at Vicksburg.

Although there is no record of either Orion or his brother ever keeping a diary, the diary entries are authentic representations of what they might have written. The book concludes with an afterword, a poem written in 1863 about Orion's courage, a bibliography, and additional children's books about drummer boys and the Civil War.

Booktalk

I was just ten years old, but as soon as I heard the call for drummer boys to serve in the Civil War, I hurried to enlist. The drum was heavy. The sun was hot. The wind, the rain, and the mud were cold. In battle, men were brave. Some screamed in pain as they were shot. Many died. But I just kept tapping the rhythmic beating of our marching pace. I kept a diary. Come. Let me tell you about it.

Curriculum Connections

Many young boys served as drummer boys not only during the Civil War but also throughout history. Have children create a K-W-L (What do we Know? What do we Want to know? What have we Learned?) chart and research more information and stories about drummer boys. Using the search engine Google, enter the descriptors: civil war drummer boys. You will find a variety of Web sites giving information about the experiences of the drummer boys of the Civil War as well as their music. Based on their readings, have children create biographical sketches and retell the stories of the drummer boys they learned about.

Citra, Becky. **Ellie's New Home**. Custer, WA: Orca, 2000. 112p. $4.50. ISBN 1-55143-164-5.

■ **CHAPTER BOOK—Nineteenth Century**
■ **AGES 7–11**

Summary

The time was 1835. Ellie, Max, and Papa sailed from England to Montreal then drove a horse-drawn wagon into the wilderness to their new homestead. Ellie and Max stayed with a neighboring family while Papa cleared some land and built a shanty. It was hard for Ellie to be brave, but by the time Papa returned, Ellie had accepted her new home and friends.

Booktalk

It was 1835. Papa told Ellie to be brave, but she was frightened and lonely. She feared that something would happen to Papa and that he would not return. The stormy night that Trevor got sick, Ellie went with Mary through the forest to get the doctor. That night was a turning point for Ellie. It was the night that she became Ellie of Canada.

Curriculum Connections

Ellie's bravery and the difficulty she had being brave when she was frightened and lonely are the themes of this book and are a good resource for character education and discussions of courage. Engage the children in a discussion of bravery. Talk about Ellie's fear, bravery, and her difficulties. Then tell an anecdote about your own fear, bravery, and difficulties and ask children to share their personal stories. In Ellie's case it was caring about someone else that pulled her out of her loneliness and enabled her to be brave. Share with the children the qualities or characteristics that enabled you to be brave. Ask the children to think about and then share the qualities or characteristics that enabled them to be brave.

Cuyler, Margery. **The Battlefield Ghost**. New York: Scholastic Press, 1999. 95p. $15.95. ISBN 0-590-19848-4.

- ■ **CHAPTER BOOK**
- ■ **AGES 7–10**

Summary

John, his sister, Lisa, and their parents move into a 300-year-old house that is haunted by the ghost of a Hessian soldier who longs to be reunited with his horse. With the help of John and Lisa, the soldier and his horse are reunited and take part in the ghostly reenactment of the battle in which they died. The "Historical Note" at the end of the book gives information about the role the Hessians played in the Revolutionary War.

Booktalk

Do you believe in ghosts? John and Lisa's house is more than 300 years old. People say it is haunted. John senses a ghost as he plays the piano and feels a light touch on his fingers. The next day Lisa feels as if someone is pushing her when she enters the first horse stall in the barn. Even Mom thinks there is a strange feeling in the barn. Could the rumors be true?

Curriculum Connections

This book might serve as a springboard to researching additional information about mercenary soldiers or reading about the Revolutionary War. After researching and reading, students might write a letter to a family member from the soldiers' viewpoint and describe life during the Revolutionary War. Create a parallel story chart that traces the events of John and Lisa's story and the events of the Hessian soldier's story.

Gerrard, Roy. **Wagons West!** New York: Farrar, Straus & Giroux, 2000. Unpaged. $5.95. ISBN 0-374-48210-1.

■ **PICTURE BOOK—Verse**
■ **AGES 7–10**

Summary

Through verse and folk art illustrations, little people tell the story of settlers traveling west to Oregon in 1850.

Booktalk

Buckskin Dan said it would be grand. The land in Oregon was rich, fertile. Food was plentiful. All the hard times would disappear. But Oregon was 2,000 miles away, and the only way to get there was by wagon train.

Curriculum Connections

Read aloud. Divide children into groups. Assign verses to each group. Have the children practice and reread as a choral reading. You can also use this book in conjunction with a social studies unit on the westward movement, in particular the Oregon Trail.

Hicyllmaz, Gaye. **Smiling for Strangers**. New York: Farrar, Straus & Giroux, 2000. 152p. $16.00. ISBN 0-374-37081-8.

- **CHAPTER BOOK—1990s; Bosnia**
- **AGES 10–14**

Summary

Fourteen-year-old Nina lives with her grandfather on the veranda of their mountain home in Bosnia as civil war rages in Yugoslavia. When her cousin returns, Nina's grandfather insists that it is time for her to leave. As Nina travels across Europe to England in the back of a convoy truck, she is filled with questions about her parents' friend to whose home she is going. When she discovers that her parents' friend, Paul, is the father of her older brother, she is shocked and angry.

Booktalk

Grandpa said to go, to "choose someone to ask, someone whom you think will say yes." With that, fourteen-year-old Nina left her mountain home. She went up the track, past the landslide, past the remains of the bridge, to the edge of the forest, and into a ditch behind a bramble patch. Below her the aid convoy stopped. She watched until she spotted the red-haired man who looked as if he would say yes.

The plan was working! Nina lost count of the days as the truck bounced along the roads. Nina had many questions as she continued her journey to safety and her parents' friend. Who was this friend? Why were the pictures and tickets in her grandmother's jacket pocket along with the letters to her mother? Why had her parents never talked about this friend? Why did her grandfather believe that she would find safety with this friend? But most of all, Nina wondered, would he be pleased to see her?

Curriculum Connections

This is a book that can be related to events and places in the news. Use a map to locate Yugoslavia and the places mentioned in the book. Trace Nina's route from Yugoslavia to Trieste, Italy, across Europe to England, then to Birmingham, and finally to Sussex.

Attention is given to decisions that Nina made: her decision to leave the past behind, her decision to love England, her decisions to ask for the help that she needed. When she met Paul, Nina decided that she did not like him. She changed her decision when she realized that Paul was very much like the brother she loved. Discuss the impact of decisions in our lives. To stimulate discussion, ask questions such as: Did you ever decide to do or not do something or to like or dislike someone or something? Did you later change your mind about doing or not doing, about liking or disliking? What happened then?

Isaacs, Anne. **Torn Thread**. New York: Scholastic Press, 2000. 192p. $15.95. ISBN 0-590-60363-9.

- ■ **CHAPTER BOOK—World War II; Jews**
- ■ **AGES 10 and up**

Summary

After the Nazi soldiers took Rachel away, Papa learned that she had been sent to a labor camp for Jewish girls and women. He arranged for twelve-year-old Eva to join her, believing that Eva would be safer with her sister in eastern Czechoslovakia than in their small town in Poland. For two years Eva and Rachel worked in the textile factory, surviving hunger and illness, until World War II ended and Russian soldiers liberated their camp.

The author has written a fictionalized account of the experiences of her mother-in-law and aunt. The names of the sisters and the names of places are real. An epilogue tells what happened to the sisters after the war ended. An afterword tells a short story and history of the camp, the factory, and the European theater of World War II.

Booktalk

"Ask yourself which choice might keep Rachel and you alive for one more hour," said Papa. The next day, Papa took Eva to the train station and sent her to the labor camp to join her sister, Rachel. For two years Eva looked after her sickly sister while the two girls worked in the textile factory staffed by Jewish girls and women. What kinds of choices do you think Eva made throughout the trials of her imprisonment and forced labor?

Curriculum Connections

Use this book in conjunction with a study of the Holocaust. If you have a Holocaust Museum in your community, you may want to visit that museum either before or after reading this book, or visit the Web site of the United States Holocaust Memorial Museum (http://www .ushmm.org).

Kacer, Kathy. **The Secret of Gabi's Dresser**. Custer, WA: Orca, 2000. 126p. $4.95. ISBN 1-896764-15-0.

- **CHAPTER BOOK—World War II; Jews**
- **AGES 10–14**

Summary

The author tells the story of her mother's experiences as a young Jewish girl in Czechoslovakia during the German occupation of World War II. Gabi, the protagonist, is now a grandmother telling her story to her grandchildren. The "Author's Note" at the end of the book tells a brief story of Gabi and the dresser, shows several pictures of Gabi, and concludes with a time line of the war in Czechoslovakia.

Booktalk

Little by little Gabi's life changed. Friends began to pull away from her and her family. Children began to cruelly taunt and tease Gabi and the other Jewish children. The Jewish teacher disappeared. Then the government appointed a "national supervisor" to run the farm. The farmworkers quit. Shopkeepers stopped selling to Jews. Jewish children were reassigned to a Jewish school. All Jews were required to wear a yellow Star of David. Then one day the Jewish school was closed. In the midst of all of this, Papa died of heart failure.

Word came that soldiers were taking young girls away from their homes. Mamma insisted that Gabi either be sent away or find a place to hide. Gabi begged to stay with Mamma and suggested that she could hide in the dresser. The day the soldiers came, Mamma locked Gabi in the dresser and clutched the key in her hand.

Curriculum Connections

This book is based on a family story about World War II. Gabi was fearful until she felt Papa's closeness and heard the reassuring words of his poem. Ask students if they have family stories about World War II. Fear and reassurance by a loved one were common experiences. Encourage them to ask family and friends for stories that they might share with their classmates or group.

You might also share an experience of a time when you were fearful until you felt the closeness of someone who loved you. Ask the children to share their experiences of being fearful until they felt the closeness of someone who loved them.

Korman, Susan. **Horse Raid**. Norwalk, CT: Soundprints, 1998. 32p. Illustrated by Bill Farnsworth. $14.95. ISBN 1-56899-613-6.

■ **PICTURE BOOK—Nineteenth Century**
■ **AGES 9–12**

Summary

When Kevin, Lucy, Tomas, and Emma visit the Smithsonian Museum's early-nineteenth-century Arapaho exhibit, Kevin suddenly finds himself transported back in time to an Arapaho camp. The women are putting up their tepees while the men hunt buffalo. Kevin, who has become Yellow Bear, helps the men when they return from the hunt. He joins in the feast and plays games with the boys. When the men plan a horse raid on a nearby Comanche camp, Yellow Bear asks and receives permission from the war leader to join them. He successfully steals a horse that he gives to his cousin who recently lost one. Then, just as suddenly as Kevin was transported to the Arapaho camp, Yellow Bear becomes Kevin and he is transported back to his friends at the Smithsonian Museum.

Booktalk

Imagine visiting the Smithsonian Museum's early-nineteenth-century Arapaho exhibit with your friends. The next thing you know, you find yourself in the midst of an Arapaho camp. The women are putting up the tepees. The men are just returning from a buffalo hunt. Someone calls, "Yellow Bear! Yellow Bear!" That's you! Now you begin your life as an Arapaho.

Curriculum Connections

Examine the roles of men and women in the Arapaho camp. Have students list the jobs of men and woman. Then have them draw pictures that show life in the camp and the jobs that men and women did.

Machlin, Mikki. **My Name Is Not Gussie.** Boston: Houghton Mifflin, 1999. 30p. $16.00. ISBN 0-395-95646-3.

■ **PICTURE BOOK—Early 1900s; Russian Jewish Immigrants**
■ **AGES 8–12**

Summary

The author retells and illustrates the stories that her mother told to her about her immigrant childhood. Each two-page spread is a story and an illustration, beginning with the family leaving Russia, crossing the ocean in steerage, and arriving at Ellis Island where Mama and the sick baby are chalked and sent into quarantine. Stories continue with Papa meeting the family, taking them home to the tenement apartment he has rented, and everyone entering into daily life in New York until finally Mama and the baby rejoin them.

Booktalk

My name was Golda until I left Russia. On Ellis Island the inspector gave me the name Augusta. That's why my name is not Gussie. The inspector said I was lucky. Had it been winter he'd have named me February. By the time we arrived on Ellis Island after the long journey from Russia, my baby sister Molly was sick. Mama and Molly were chalked and sent into quarantine. But Papa was there to meet us and took the rest of us, Tante Feindele, Uncle Itzhak, Cousin Heike, my two older brothers, and me, home to the railroad apartment he had rented. A railroad apartment is a long row of rooms with one window in the front and one window in the back. That's where my life began as a Jewish immigrant girl in New York City in the early 1900s.

Curriculum Connections

What was life like in the early 1900s? Begin with information given in this book, and then expand by using other sources such as those listed in "Related Books." Identify topics of interest such as transportation, immigration, clothing, and others.

Related Books

Another story of Russian Jewish immigrants in the early 1900s is *The Memory Coat*, which is reviewed in this section. *Town Mouse House: How We Lived One Hundred Years Ago, One-Room School, Girls: A History of Growing Up Female in America*, and *The Century That Was* are reviewed in this chapter and give information about life in the early 1900s.

Myers, Anna. **Captain's Command**. New York: Walker, 1999. 144p. $15.95. ISBN 0-8027-8706-1.

- ■ **CHAPTER BOOK—World War II**
- ■ **AGES 10 and up**

Summary

It was almost Christmas of 1943 when Gail and her family learned that Daddy was missing in action. Mamma held fast to her belief that Daddy was not dead although Uncle Ned, most of the townspeople, and even Daddy's grandma, Big Mama, believed that he had been killed. The author tells two parallel stories: one the story of the injured navigator and gunner in Occupied France, the other the story of Gail and her family in Oklahoma.

Booktalk

The injured navigator pulled the injured gunner from the burning B-17. Were they over Germany or over Occupied France when they were hit? If they were in Occupied France, they had a chance. In the distance were voices, one French, the other German. The navigator began to move toward the ditch pulling the gunner along with him.

In another country, Gail was almost home from school when she saw George Rogers leaving their house. George delivered telegrams. Mama held the telegram in her hand. She screamed and then she cried. Daddy was missing in action.

While Gail and her family got ready for Christmas, the navigator pulled the gunner to the safety of a cornfield where French resistance fighters found them. The navigator's wounds healed but the gunner died. After the navigator and the French resistance fighters buried the gunner, the navigator managed to make his way back to the safety of England. On Christmas Eve Gail and her family received news of Daddy. What was the news? Was Gail's daddy dead or alive?

Curriculum Connections

Explore life on the home front during World War II after reading this book. Music of the time, patriotism, rationing, savings stamps and bonds, victory gardens, women factory workers, and shortages of foods, gas, rubber tires, and fabrics were all part of the way of life. Most families had a family member fighting in the war. Many family members or friends were injured, missing in action, or killed.

Talk about life on the home front as presented in the book, make a list, then have children develop questions to ask grandparents and great-grandparents. You might have children visit a senior center, a senior residence, or a retirement home to carry on conversations about the World War II years. Retell the stories that children gather by making a chart or book.

Osborne, Mary Pope. **Adaline Falling Star**. New York: Scholastic Press, 2000. 170p. $16.95. ISBN 0-439-05947-X.

- **CHAPTER BOOK—Nineteenth Century; Native Americans; African Americans**
- **AGES 9–14**

Summary

Kit Carson had an Arapaho daughter named Adaline Falling Star. Little is known of the real Adaline Falling Star Carson. This story is a fictionalized account of what her experiences might have been while she lived with relatives in St. Louis. It authentically reflects the attitudes of white people toward Native Americans and African Americans in the 1840s.

Booktalk

Adaline and the stray dog that is her travel companion are traveling upriver in search of her father when debris from an exploding steamboat hits Adaline in the forehead. Now what? Her mother is dead. Cousin Silas and his family don't like her. John Fremont said that her father, Kit Carson, went on to New Mexico when the expedition ended. The stray dog has once saved Adaline from drowning. Will he save her again? Will Adaline find her father? If she does, will he want her?

Curriculum Connections

Although a fictional story, this book is an authentic representation of frontier life and early St. Louis in the 1840s. Have students research and report on Native American life, attitudes toward Native Americans, slavery on the western frontier, explorations, tall tales, early steamboats, life on the Mississippi, frontier life, and life in early St. Louis.

Ransom, Candice F. **The Promise Quilt**. New York: Walker, 1999. 32p. $16.95. ISBN 0-8027-8694-4.

- ■ **PICTURE BOOK—Civil War Era**
- ■ **AGES 5–8**

Summary

Before he left to serve as General Lee's guide during the Civil War, Addie's Papa promised her that she would go to school to learn to read and write when she was older. When the war ended, Addie and her family learned that Papa had died. Because soldiers had destroyed the school, Addie's mother made a quilt to raffle for money to buy books. Mr. Brown offered his shed as a school and Papa's promise was fulfilled. The "Author's Note" at the end of the book gives a short history of the Civil War.

Booktalk

When I was little, Papa promised me that I could go to school to learn to read and write when I got older. Then the war came. We had no money and we had no school. But Mama said, "Maybe we'll find a way." The lady told Mama to make a quilt to be raffled for money. Mama cut and sewed until she had no fabric left. She couldn't finish the quilt. Could we still find a way?

Curriculum Connections

How did life in the Southern states change as a result of the Civil War? Begin with information given in this book.

Related Books

Read and research using other sources such as Irene Hunt's *Across Five Aprils*.

Van Steenwyk, Elizabeth. **A Traitor Among Us**. Grand Rapids, MI: Eerdmans Books for Young Readers, 1998. 133p. $15.00. ISBN 0-8028-5150-9.

■ **CHAPTER BOOK—World War II; Netherlands**
■ **AGES 9–12**

Summary

Pieter's constant fear and the courageous decisions and actions that he takes in spite of his fear are the ongoing theme of this book. This fictional story set in a fictional town in the Netherlands during the autumn of 1944 is based on real events and the experiences of real people.

Booktalk

Thirteen-year-old Pieter lives with his mother in a small village in the southeastern corner of the Netherlands. It is the autumn of 1944 during World War II and the Nazis occupy the Netherlands. Fear has been Pieter's constant companion since the Nazis took his father away from his bed in the wee hours of the morning. The Nazis even took Pieter's dog. His brothers are fighting with the Resistance.

Now it seems there is a traitor in the village. It could be anyone— the schoolteacher, the doctor, a friend, a neighbor, even a relative. Thirteen-year-old Pieter trusts his friend, Jan, and of course, Beppie. But should he? Pieter believes that he knows the identity of the traitor. Now he must expose him.

Curriculum Connections

Engage children in a discussion of Pieter's constant fear and the courageous decisions and actions that he took in spite of his fear. Why was Pieter afraid? Did he act on his fear? What courageous decisions did he make? What courageous actions did he take? What might have happened had he acted on his fear rather than his courage? Would the outcomes have been the same? Brainstorm and generate a list of names of historic people who acted on courage rather then fear such as Harriet

Tubman and Abraham Lincoln. How might history be different if these people had acted on fear instead? Then, ask students to recall their own or others' experiences, as well as experiences derived from reading or the media (television, radio, newspapers, magazines, movies). What choices and actions were taken based on courage? What choices and actions were taken based on fear? Create a chart listing choices and actions based on courage and on fear. Extend the activity by gathering news stories that demonstrate courage in the face of fear. Create a bulletin board of the news stories. Identify the choices and actions taken. This book can also be used to launch a discussion of suspicion, trust, and betrayal.

Woodruff, Elvira. **The Memory Coat**. New York: Scholastic Press, 1999. Unpaged. $15.95. ISBN 0-590-67717-9.

- ■ **PICTURE BOOK—Early 1900s; Russian Jewish Immigrants**
- ■ **AGES 7–10**

Summary

This is the story of Jewish life in Russia in the early 1900s, the hard journey of Russian Jewish immigrants by wagon and train through Europe, and the fourteen-day ocean crossing in which Jews frequently were relegated to steerage class. The final challenge was entry through Ellis Island. The "Author's Note" and "Historical Notes" at the back of the book retell the story of the author's visit to Ellis Island and her inspiration for writing this book.

Booktalk

Grisha's coat was becoming ragged and tattered, covered with patches, but he would not let Aunt Bubba make him a new coat. His mother had made the coat for him shortly before she died. Grisha could not part with it.

When Grisha and his family left Russia for America, they traveled by wagon and train through Europe, and then across the ocean in steerage class. Would they be allowed to enter America once they arrived at Ellis Island? They knew that immigrants who were poor or unhealthy were marked with chalk and turned back. So many things could go wrong—and they did.

Would Grisha have to return to Russia? What about his family? Would they stay in America or return to Russia with Grisha?

Curriculum Connections

Engage children in a discussion of their own families' origins and immigration to America. Encourage Native American children to tell their native stories of how their people came to be in this land. Create a map of the families' origins and immigration routes. Have children trace their families' journeys and tell their stories.

Related Books

Another book about Russian Jewish immigrants in the early 1900s is *My Name Is Not Gussie* and is reviewed in this section.

PLACES

Cobb, Vicki. **This Place Is Wild: East Africa.** New York: Walker, 1998. 32p. Illustrated by Barbara Lavallee. $7.95. ISBN 0-8027-7579-9.

■ **PICTURE BOOK**
■ **AGES 7–12**

Summary

Illustrations and text introduce readers to the wild game of East Africa and to the Masai people that live there.

Booktalk

Imagine riding in a Land Rover across the game preserves of Kenya and Uganda in East Africa. What do you think you would see? (Let the children respond, and prompt with the following.) Elephants? Giraffes? Ostriches? Antelope and gazelles? Zebra? How about lions, cheetahs, and leopards? And rhinos?

What about people? Would you see people on the plains? Perhaps. One group of people who make their homes there are the Masai. What is life like for the Masai? Can you imagine living there?

Curriculum Connections

Respond to the title of the series, Imagine Living Here, by having the children imagine living in East Africa. Have them brainstorm, create a semantic web, and then create shoe box dioramas that show the land, vegetation, animals, and people of East Africa as presented in this book.

Related Books

Other titles in the Imagine Living Here Series are printed on the back cover of this book.

Myers, Christopher. **Black Cat.** New York: Scholastic Press, 1999. Unpaged. $16.95. ISBN 0-590-03375-1.

■ **PICTURE BOOK—Verse**
■ **AGES 7 and up**

Summary

Christopher Myers, Caldecott Honor Book artist and son of Walter Dean Myers, gives us a powerful picture book of rhythmic free verse and bold collage illustrated with photographs taken in Harlem. Urban children will recognize their world and their experiences as the black cat explores its neighborhood.

Booktalk/Read-Aloud

Read aloud and show the pictures. This is a book to be seen as well as heard.

Curriculum Connections

After reading aloud and showing the pictures, encourage children to create additional cat scenarios from their own neighborhoods and communities.

Vieira, Linda. **Grand Canyon: A Trail Through Time**. New York: Walker, 2000. 34p. Illustrated by Christopher Canyon. $7.95. ISBN 0-8027-7569-1.

- ■ **PICTURE BOOK**
- ■ **AGES 5–8**

Summary

Brilliantly colored illustrations depict the ever-changing colors of the Grand Canyon, and informative text weaves the formation and history into an account of a typical day at the Grand Canyon.

Booktalk/Bookwalk

(This is a book to be seen. Show the pictures with the booktalk.) Lightning flashes across the sky. It is early morning along the rim of the Grand Canyon (pages 4–5). As dawn breaks, coyotes teach their pups to hunt for food (pages 6–7). Tourists come to view the Canyon (pages 8–9). As the sun climbs into the sky, the Colorado River comes into view (pages 10–11). Pack mules pick their way along the twisting trail to the riverbed below (pages 12–13). Visitors can see the symbols painted long ago by the Havasupai Indians who still live in the Grand Canyon (pages 14–15). Bighorn sheep and wildflowers live along the steep rocky walls of the Canyon (pages 16–17). Mules continue down the trail (pages 18–19) past a granary built 1,000 years ago by Anasazi Indians (pages 20–21), with lizards and fossils (pages 22–23), cacti and a white-breasted nuthatch (pages 24–25), to the bunkhouse along the river's edge (pages 26–27). The sun sets (pages 28–29) and the mules rest before making the seven-hour trip back to the rim (pages 30–31).

Curriculum Connections

Use the time lines in the front and back of the book as models to reconstruct classroom time lines showing the rock formations of the Grand Canyon and the history of human settlement and exploration in and around the Canyon. Construct split-twig animal figures like those of the earliest Indians (see Appendix B).

RELATIONSHIPS AND COMING OF AGE

Brisson, Pat. **The Summer My Father Was Ten**. Honesdale, PA: Boyds Mills Press, 1998. Unpaged. Illustrated by Andrea Shine. $8.95. ISBN 1-56397-435-5.

- ■ **PICTURE BOOK—Fiction**
- ■ **AGES 5–10**

Summary

Impressionistic watercolors punctuated with a spattering of pointillism illustrate this touching story of a young boy's attempt to make amends when he and his friends destroy the garden of an elderly neighbor. The story is told from the point of view of a young girl who retells the story told by her father.

Booktalk

Have you ever accidentally destroyed something when you were playing? That's what my dad did. Every spring while we plant our garden, my dad tells me the same story of what happened when he was a boy. He and his friends were only playing. They didn't mean to destroy old Mr. Bellavista's garden, but they did. When Mr. Bellavista interrupted their play, my dad looked at the trampled garden and he knew that he wanted to say, "I'm sorry." But he couldn't. He just couldn't. What could he do?

Curriculum Connections

Encourage the children to find out about and retell family stories. This is also a good opportunity to encourage the children to talk about their own experiences of doing something for which they wanted to say "I'm sorry" and to describe how they felt. How did they manage to apologize? How did they feel when they did apologize? What happened after they said I'm sorry?

Choyce, Lesley. **Carrie's Crowd**. Custer, WA: Orca, 1998. 64p. Illustrated by Mark Thurman. $3.99. ISBN 0-88780-464-0.

- ■ **CHAPTER BOOK—Friends**
- ■ **AGES 8–11**

Summary

Nine short, easy-to-read chapters tell the story of Carrie, who learns a lesson about friendship when she tries to gain acceptance from a cool group of children.

Booktalk

Carrie decided to be cool like Giselle and Kirsten. No more rollerblading or hanging out with Laura who just wants to read about space. Then Mom said it was time to go shopping for some clothes. This was Carrie's chance to change her image and even get a new haircut. She didn't really like the Smartgirls music, but Giselle and Kirsten did. Carrie could hardly believe it when Giselle chose her to be her best friend. But all of that changed at Giselle's birthday party.

Curriculum Connections

This book lends itself to a discussion of friendship. What are the qualities that we look for in friends? How did Giselle and Kirsten act like friends? How did they not act like friends? What did Carrie learn about friendship?

Related Books

Carrie's Crowd is the second book about Carrie in the First Novels Series. Other books in the series are listed with brief annotations at the back of the book. The thirty-nine titles listed include the first book about Carrie, *Go for It, Carrie*; two books about Morgan: *Morgan and the Money* and *Morgan Makes Magic*; and two books about Jan: *Jan and Patch* and *Jan's Big Bang*.

Crunk, Tony. **Big Mama**. New York: Farrar, Straus & Giroux, 2000. Unpaged. Illustrated by Margot Apple. $16.00. ISBN 0-374-30688-5.

■ **PICTURE BOOK—Families**
■ **AGES 5–8**

Summary

The neighborhood children like to play at Billy's house. His grandma, Big Mama, can make a freight train, a space capsule, or a mule wagon. She can talk backwards and play kickball. Best of all are the adventures the children have walking with her from her house to the ice-cream stand and back again.

Booktalk

Come on! Let's go to Big Mama's house. Big Mama—that's Billy's grandma—is cool! We can camp out in her living room, play submarine around her kitchen table, and even crawl to the center of the earth under her back porch. You won't believe all the things she can do! Do you know she can even talk backwards? Do you know anyone like Big Mama?

Curriculum Connection

Have the children retell part of the story by drawing a map that shows the path that Billy and his friends took from Big Mama's house to Woody's ice-cream stand and home again.

Delacre, Lulu. **Salsa Stories**. New York: Scholastic Press, 2000. 104p. $15.95. ISBN 0-590-63118-7.

■ **CHAPTER BOOK—Short Stories; Latin America; ESOL; Catholic**
■ **AGES 9 and up**

Summary

Seven short stories followed by a recipe book of the foods that occurred in the stories, a Spanish-English glossary, and a family tree of Carmen Teresa's family and friends all enhanced by black-and-white drawings complete this little book.

Booktalk

When Dona Josefa gives Carmen Teresa a blank notebook as a New Year's gift, Carmen Teresa has no idea what to write about. Then Mama suggests that Carmen Teresa collect stories from family members and friends. Flor, Abuelito, Abuelita, Abita, Uncle Robert, Dona Josefa, and Tia Marilia each tell a story about a childhood celebration. Now Carmen Teresa has a different idea about what to write in her blank book.

Curriculum Connections

Introduce the book by preparing and serving one of the recipes, such as Sesame Drink, Coconut Sherbet, Carmel Sandwich Cookies, or Coconut Kisses, included at the end of the book. Have students collect childhood celebration stories and recipes from family members and friends and compile their own books.

Related Books

Additional books by the author retell myths, legends, folktales, songs, and rhymes from Latin America and are listed inside the back cover of this book.

Freeman, Marcia S. **Catfish and Spaghetti**. Gainesville, FL: Maupin House, 1998. 50p. Illustrated by Rose Stock. $4.50. ISBN 0-929895-21-5.

■ **CHAPTER BOOK—Families**
■ **AGES 8–12**

Summary

Kerry tries selling worms to earn enough money to buy a rod and reel. She finds no more than a dozen at a time until Mr. Hager teaches her how to fiddle for worms. Fiddling for worms means pounding a board into the dirt and rubbing a cinder block back and forth across it. The wiggling and screeching of the board draws the worms out of the ground. By fiddling for worms, Kerry earns enough money to buy the rod and reel she uses to catch the big catfish.

Booktalk

Money was tight. Kerry loved to fish and she tried to help her family by fishing for the evening meal. Kerry knew that she could catch the big catfish that she saw swimming near the bridge if only she had a rod and reel instead of a pole and line.

But selling worms wasn't easy money. Even though she dug in the yard, scratched in the compost pile, and her mother took her night crawling, Kerry found no more than a dozen worms to sell at any one time. Then Mr. Hager taught her how to fiddle for worms.

Curriculum Connections

In this story set in Florida, the author describes the custom of fiddling for worms that she learned as a child. Use this story as a springboard for children to question family members and friends about customs and practices from their childhoods. Prepare a book written as a journal or anthology of childhood customs and practices of family and friends. You might also present the children with the following mathematics problem:

How many worms must you sell at five cents apiece in order to earn $39.99, the price of a rod and reel?

Jones, Jennifer B. **Dear Mrs. Ryan, You're Ruining My Life**. New York: Walker, 2000. 132p. $15.95. ISBN 0-8027-8728-2.

- ■ **CHAPTER BOOK**
- ■ **AGES 10 and up**

Summary

Harvey is embarrassed by his mom, a children's book writer, who includes anecdotes about Harvey and his fifth-grade friends in her books. Harvey's life gets even more embarrassing when his mom starts dating his school principal.

Booktalk

Harvey's mom writes children's books. She includes stories about Harvey and his friends. How embarrassing! Maybe if she would start dating . . . Harvey and his friends plot to get his mom together with

Mr. Stevenson, the school principal. Unfortunately, it works. Now life is even more embarrassing for Harvey.

Curriculum Connections

This book lends itself to a discussion of problem solving, solutions, and problem-solving strategies. Discuss Harvey's problems, solutions, and problem-solving strategies. Then ask children what kinds of problems they have had to solve and what strategies they used. Make a problem-solving chart starting with Harvey, his problems, and his problem-solving strategies. Continue with the children, their problems, and their problem-solving strategies.

Mack, Tracy. **Drawing Lessons**. New York: Scholastic Press, 2000. 168p. $15.95. ISBN 0-439-11202-8.

- **CHAPTER BOOK—Families**
- **AGES 10 and up**

Summary

The story of Rory who wanted to be an artist like her dad (but she stopped drawing and painting when her parents separated) is fully developed in Chapter 4, in the section "Art."

McCully, Emily Arnold. **Monk Camps Out**. New York: Arthur A. Levine Books, 2000. Unpaged. $15.95. ISBN 0-439-09976-5.

- **PICTURE BOOK—Families**
- **AGES 6–10**

Summary

Monk, the little mouse, decides to camp out with only a little help from his parents. They help him as he struggles to put up the tent in the backyard. They pack a lunch for Monk's dinner, and then go outside to give him a good night hug when the dark comes. During the night, Monk creeps into the house through the front door, curls up in Mom's chair, and goes back to sleep. Meanwhile, Monk's parents slip out the back door, peek into the dark tent, lie down on the ground, and go to sleep. In the morning they find each other but doze off to sleep at the breakfast table. Cartoon-like illustrations enliven the text.

Booktalk

When Monk, the little mouse, announced to his parents that he was going to camp out, they helped only a little. They gave only a little help as he struggled to put up his tent. They packed only a little lunch for Monk's dinner, and only went out to give him a little good night hug when the dark came. Now when morning has come, Monk is not in his tent and his parents are not in their beds. Where are they?

Curriculum Connections

Read aloud and position the book for all to see. Use a pointer and encourage the children to follow along. Engage children in conversation about campouts, sleepovers, and helpful families. Invite children to share stories about how their families are helpful and how they look out for them just like Monk's parents helped and looked out for Monk.

Related Books

See McCully's *Mouse Practice*, which is included in Chapter 4, in the section "Sports," for another story about Monk.

Meddaugh, Susan. **The Best Place**. Boston: Houghton Mifflin, 1999. Unpaged. $15.00. ISBN 0-395-97994-3.

■ **PICTURE BOOK—Friends**
■ **AGES 6–10**

Summary

The wolf thinks his screen porch is the best place in the whole world until the bird points out that the wolf hasn't traveled to any other place. So the wolf sells his house and sets out to see the world. From the jungle to the desert to the city of London, he still thinks his screen porch the best place. So, he returns home and begs the rabbit family to let him buy back his house. When they refuse, he has a terrible temper tantrum. He tries to make amends by preparing a dinner party for the rabbit family but only frightens all of the neighbors who believe that the rabbits will be the dinner. The animals chase the wolf deep into the forest where he climbs high into a tree and falls asleep. When the wolf awakes the next morning, he discovers the most beautiful sight he has ever seen and determines to build his new home in the tree. Meanwhile, the animals discover the dinner that the wolf had prepared and realize their mistake. When the animals find the wolf deep in the forest, they help him build his new home.

Booktalk

Do you have a favorite place? The wolf did. He thought his screen porch was the best place in the whole world. He even traveled the world to find a better place. What did he find? Well, it wasn't the view that made the new place the very best in the world. (Discuss the ending when the wolf says that he's found the best place in the world, the bird agrees that the view is indeed beautiful, and the wolf replies, "That's not what makes it best.")

Curriculum Connections

Children might want to talk about what it is to throw a tantrum, lose one's friends, be misunderstood, and then regain one's friends. Talk about the importance of having friends and belonging to a community. Have children make a chart that lists the importance of friends and community and draw pictures to illustrate the items on the chart.

Mills, Claudia. **Gus and Grandpa Ride the Train.** New York: Farrar, Straus & Giroux, 1998. 48p. $4.95. ISBN 0-374-42813-1.

- **CHAPTER BOOK—Families**
- **AGES 5–8**

Summary

This book is an easy reader with three chapters that tell about Gus who loves to wave at the trains when he visits his grandpa, the train set in Grandpa's attic that belonged to Gus's daddy when he was a boy, and the train ride that Gus and Grandpa take together.

Booktalk

Gus loves to wave at the trains that pass by when he visits his grandpa and to play with the train set that belonged to Gus's daddy when he was a little boy. One day Gus and Grandpa even go for a ride on a real train. But when Gus forgets to close the gate, Grandpa's dog Skipper gets loose. And when Grandpa looks in his wallet and his pocket, the train tickets are not there. What do you suppose Gus and Grandpa do?

Curriculum Connections

Talk with the children about what Gus and Grandpa did together. Ask children if they have a grandparent, aunt, uncle, or special adult that they like to do things with. Brainstorm a list of activities that the children like to do with a special adult. Have each child write a sentence and draw a picture about what they like to do with that person.

Related Books

Other titles in the Gus and Grandpa Early Reader Series are *Gus and Grandpa and the Christmas Cookies*, *Gus and Grandpa at the Hospital*, and *Gus and Grandpa and the Two-Wheeled Bike*.

Nickle, John. **The Ant Bully.** New York: Scholastic Press, 1999. Unpaged. $14.95. ISBN 0-590-39591-2.

- ■ **PICTURE BOOK—Fiction**
- ■ **AGES 5–8**

Summary

Sid bullies Lucas so Lucas bullies the ants. The ants get even with Lucas by pulling him into their ant hole where he is sentenced to hard labor with worker ants.

Booktalk

It was because of Sid, the neighborhood bully, that Lucas squirted his water pistol at the ants on the sidewalk. The next thing he knows the ants are stuffing Lucas down their ant hole and into their Queen's chamber.

The Queen is very angry with Lucas for flooding and destroying her colony. She orders the Ant Wizard to shrink Lucas and bring him to trial where he is found guilty and sentenced to hard labor with the worker ants. Is this how Lucas will spend the rest of his life—a very, very small boy among all of these ants? No, wait, there's hope. He can return to his life as a full-sized boy providing he passes the test that the Queen sets for him.

Curriculum Connections

Lucas discovered what it was to be very, very small. Speedy and Rene, his ant friends, wanted to know what it was like to be a giant. Divide the children into two groups. Have one group be very, very small like ants. Have the other group be giants like Lucas and Sid. Start with information in the book, expand upon it by brainstorming, and have each group discuss among themselves then share with the other group what it is to be very, very small or to be a giant. What do they see? What do they feel? What would they eat? Where would they go?

Extend this book into a science lesson by setting up and observing an ant colony.

Rylant, Cynthia. **Poppleton in Fall**. New York: Blue Sky Press, 1999. 48p. Illustrated by Mark Teague. $14.95. ISBN 0-590-84789-9.

- **CHAPTER BOOK—Friends**
- **AGES 5–8**

Summary

The Poppleton books are a series of chapter books for beginning readers. Each book consists of three chapters. Each chapter is a self-contained story about the daily life experiences of Poppleton the pig, Cherry Sue the goat, and their talking animal friends. In each chapter, Poppleton has a problem that Cherry Sue solves.

In the first chapter of this book, Poppleton is sad when his duck friends flies south, so he goes to visit Cherry Sue, who suggests that he take a nap. In the second chapter, Poppleton is depressed because Zacko the ferret cannot make a coat big enough to fit Poppleton. Cherry Sue suggests that Poppleton order a new coat from a catalog for Big and Tall Pigs. In the third chapter, the lion repeatedly roars "no" when Poppleton orders a plain pancake for Cherry Sue at the Lions'

Club Pancake Breakfast, so Cherry Sue changes her order to a blueberry pancake.

Booktalk

Who do you turn to when you have a problem, want comfort, or just need a friend? Poppleton the pig turns to Cherry Sue the goat. When Poppleton is sad, Cherry Sue knows how to comfort him. When Poppleton has a problem, Cherry Sue has a suggestion for solving it. And when Poppleton needs a friend, he can count on Cherry Sue. What do you think Poppleton's problem is this time? How will Cherry Sue help? Do you have a friend like Cherry Sue?

Curriculum Connections

Ask children to think about a special friend in their own lives. Has that special friend comforted them or helped them solve a problem? Encourage children to share stories about their special friends.

Related Books

Other books in the Poppleton Series listed on the back flap of the book cover are *Poppleton*, *Poppleton and Friends*, *Poppleton Everyday*, *Poppleton Forever*, and *Poppleton in Spring*.

Spalding, Andrea, and Janet Wilson. **Sarah May and the New Red Dress**. Custer, WA: Orca, 1998. Unpaged. $14.95. ISBN 1-55143-117-3.

▪ **PICTURE BOOK—Families**
▪ **AGES 3–8**

Summary

The book begins and ends with "I wasn't always Grandma . . . Once I was Sarah May." The story is about the little girl, Sarah May, whose sensible navy blue dress turns into her new red dress.

Booktalk

Before I was Grandma and was just Sarah May, I needed a new dress. I wanted a red dress but Mama made me a navy blue dress. The West Wind told me to wait. I didn't like my navy blue dress but the West Wind told me that I would. When I said that I really didn't like my navy blue dress, I heard the West Wind laughing. The West Wind was right. How do you suppose the navy blue dress that I didn't like turned into the new red dress that I wanted?

Curriculum Connections

Encourage children to ask grandparents or other older family members for stories from their childhoods. What were their favorite clothes? Did they ever have a wish granted? Have them retell their family stories.

Related Books

Other books by Andrea Spalding are *The Most Beautiful Kite in the World*, *Finders Keepers*, *An Island of My Own*, *Phoebe and the Gypsy*, and *Me and Mr. Mah* by Andrea Spalding and Janet Wilson, which is reviewed in Chapter 2, in the section "Gardens and Gardening."

Steig, William. **Pete's a Pizza**. New York: HarperCollins, 1998. Unpaged. $15.95. ISBN 0-06-20517-1.

■ **PICTURE BOOK—Families**
■ **AGES 5–8**

Summary

Pete is in a bad mood. To cheer him up, his father makes him into a pizza. After kneading, stretching, whirling, and twirling him, sprinkling him with oil (water), flour (talcum powder), tomatoes (checkers), and cheese (pieces of paper), Pete's father puts him into the oven (on the sofa) to bake. Pete runs away when it is time to be sliced, but is captured and hugged, then freed to go outside to play with his friends.

Booktalk/Bookwalk

(Show children the cover and interior illustrations as you talk.) Have you ever been turned into a pizza? Pete was. His father kneaded, stretched, whirled, and twirled him, sprinkled him with oil, flour, tomatoes, and cheese, then popped him into the oven to bake. (Continue by reading aloud and showing the pictures that correspond closely with the sparse text on each page.)

Curriculum Connections

This book is based on a game that the author played with his daughter. Engage listeners in an oral discussion of family practices and activities. Does your family play games? What does your family do to cheer you when you're in a bad mood? Have children talk with a partner then share their experiences in groups of four. Ask a spokesperson from each group of four to share with the whole group. Make a list of family practices and activities.

Wishinsky, Freida, and H. Werner Zimmerman. **Each One Special.** Custer, WA: Orca, 1998. Unpaged. $14.95. ISBN 1-55143-122-X.

■ **PICTURE BOOK**
■ **AGES 5–8**

Summary

When Harry the cake decorator retires, he needs something to do. When Ben's mom gives him some clay, Ben needs help. Ben takes his clay to Harry. Before long people come to buy their clay sculptures that are each as special as Harry's decorated cakes had been.

Booktalk

Harry was a cake decorator. Sometimes he let Ben help decorate his cakes. Harry's decorated cakes were always special and everyone loved them. Ben knew that Harry could make anything. When the bakery owner sold his shop, the new owners wanted fast, young bakers who decorated all of their cakes the same. So Harry retired and needed something to do. And Ben needed help with the clay his mother gave him. Come see what Harry and Ben make with their clay.

Curriculum Connections

Show the pictures and point out that each decorated cake and each clay sculpture is different and special. Talk about the features that make each one different and special. Then identify and talk about the attributes that make each child different and special. Pair children and have each child compose a sentence about his/her partner that says, "_____ is special because _____." Extend the book with an art lesson by giving the children clay for making sculptures like the ones Harry and Ben made, such as a bird, a cat, a rose, a daisy, and a cowboy. Remind the children that each sculpture is different and special.

CHAPTER 4

Arts and Recreation

INTRODUCTION

Picture books, junior novels, fiction, and nonfiction provide opportunities for a multitude of creative responses. These creative responses, in turn, enhance the development of literacy and retention of learning. Introduce young readers to Benjamin West, called the Father of American Art. Books can explain how jazz began in Africa and developed into the rap music that we hear today, and of the development of the orchestra and its instruments. Lullabies, jump rope rhymes, piano music of the silent movies, plus familiar compositions of "Peter and the Wolf," "The Friendly Beasts," and "Old MacDonald Had a Farm, " provide opportunities for reading, listening, and singing. Dancers will enjoy Mimi the swan who became a ballerina, Naty who danced as a mouse in the Guelaguetza parade, and Parvati who became the most talented dancer in all of India. Virginia Hamilton's retelling of Rumplestiltskin and Isaac Olaleye's retelling of a Nigerian folktale provide opportunities for acting and creative dramatics. Finally, sports lovers will enjoy meeting the baseball greats from the Negro Leagues and discovering other fascinating reads about baseball, basketball, and hockey.

ART

Brenner, Barbara. **The Boy Who Loved to Draw**. Boston: Houghton Mifflin, 1999. 48p. Illustrated by Olivier Dunrea. $15.00. ISBN 0-395-85080-0.

■ **PICTURE BOOK—Nonfiction**
■ **AGES 5–8**

Summary

Benjamin West, often called the Father of American Art, began drawing at the age of seven. He sold his first painting at the age of twelve. As an adult he studied art in Italy, then settled in England, and became well known in both Europe and America. This is his life story. Folk art illustrations similar to West's early work supplement the text.

Booktalk

More than anything else, he loved to draw. He was never without pen and notebook, and he drew nearly everything he saw. He even pulled cat hairs to make paintbrushes, and the Lenape Indians showed him how to make paint out of clay. The boy who loved to draw grew up to become a famous artist. He is known as the Father of American Art. Who is he?

Curriculum Connections

Follow up by showing slides of Benjamin West's paintings. The slides should be available in your public library collection, a nearby museum collection, or the collection of your state university library. Or you may want to set up a display of children's picture books that are illustrated in the American folk art tradition. With older readers, ask: What is folk art? Do people create folk art today? Use this book in conjunction with a study of early American folk art, a study of American art history, or a study of American artists.

Desimini, Lisa. **Sun & Moon: A Love Story**. New York: Blue Sky Press, 1999. Unpaged. $16.95. ISBN 0-590-18720-1.

■ **PICTURE BOOK—Fantasy**
■ **ALL AGES**

Summary

A girl giant and a boy giant each walk the earth, alone and lonely, she in the moonlight, he in the sunlight. Both the boy and the girl dream of someone to love until an eclipse brings them together.

Bookwalk

Retell the story by showing the book, turning the pages, and showing the pictures. Once there was a girl giant (pages 1–2) and a boy giant (pages 2–3) who walked the earth alone (pages 3–4). She bathed and slept by moonlight (pages 5–6). He bathed and slept by sunlight (pages 7–8). She collected shooting stars (page 9). He made shadow puppets (page 10). They always had something to do (pages 11–12). But they were sad (pages 13–14). Each wanted someone to love (pages 15–16). And so they dreamed until one day. . . (pages 17–18).

Curriculum Connections

Lyrical language and illustrations create a mystical quality to this romantic fantasy that is likely to appeal to all ages. Photographs, paper, fabric, hair, fruit, and paintings scanned into the computer created a collage that was used to create the images in the illustrations. This creative approach is one that readers may enjoy exploring to create their own images and illustrations either on the computer or as a traditional collage.

Mack, Tracy. **Drawing Lessons**. New York: Scholastic Press, 2000. 168p. $15.95. ISBN 0-439-11202-8.

■ **CHAPTER BOOK—Fiction**
■ **AGES 10 and up**

Summary

Rory's father is an artist. She wants to be one too. When her parents separate, Rory is hurt and angry. She feels the loss of her father and stops drawing and painting. When Rory's father comes looking for her after she takes the train back home instead of returning to her grandmother's apartment, Rory once again feels his love and presence. She discovers that through her drawing and painting she can reconnect with his presence in her life.

Note: On page 32 Rory walks into her artist father's studio to see her father kissing his nude model. There are also references to Rory and her friend Nicky deciding that it is time to begin wearing bras. There are no graphic descriptions or titillating language, but some children may be embarrassed and some parents may be offended.

Booktalk

None of us wanted to but we had to. The tree was sick and it had to come down. Rory had drawn the tree in her sketchbook. She could paint it and keep our tree forever. That is what is so great about painting.

But now that her dad's gone, Rory has stopped painting. Rory's dad is an artist and her drawing coach. Rory is hurt and angry, ashamed to tell her best friend or her art teacher that her parents have separated. Although her dad writes, he doesn't call, and he won't ever come back home. Why couldn't Mom have tried harder? If you have ever thought that you've lost someone important to you, you'll want to know how Rory brings her dad back into her life, just as she painted and kept her tree forever.

Curriculum Connections

Discuss what it is to have a gift such as drawing and painting, music, or writing—a gift that allows for self-expression and is a tool for healing. Rory describes herself as thinking in colors, seeing pictures in everything, and just knowing inside how light shifts and shapes things. Rory's friend Nicky has a gift for languages, which just seem to slip off her tongue. You may want to use this book in conjunction with the one listed in "Related Books" to explore gifts such as art, music, and dance.

Extend the book by asking children if they have ever thought they lost someone important and then found them again. This is a thought-provoking book that lends itself to a discussion of grief, loss, and forgiveness.

Related Books

Shiva's Fire, included in this chapter, is the story of a young girl with the gift of dance.

MUSIC

Chocolate, Debbi. **The Piano Man**. New York: Walker, 2000.
32p. Illustrated by Eric Velasquez. $7.95. ISBN 0-8027-7578-0.

- ■ PICTURE BOOK—Fiction; African Americans
- ■ AGES 5–8

Summary

A young girl tells the story of her grandfather who played the piano
to accompany the silent movies. He also played the piano on Broadway, for a traveling medicine show, and then with a vaudeville show
where he met the dancer who became his wife. The girl's grandparents
performed in musical comedies until her mother was born. Then Grandfather again played the piano for the silent movies. After the talkies
came out, he became a piano tuner. The piano man shared his stories
and love for music with his granddaughter and even played the music
of the silent movies for her.

Booktalk

Jelly Roll Morton taught him to play two pianos at once. Scott
Joplin taught him to play the "Maple Leaf Rag." My grandfather played
the piano for the silent movies. He played the piano on Broadway for
Mr. Ziegfield's Follies, on the road for a medicine show, and even for
vaudeville shows. That's how he met my grandmother. She was a
dancer. When my mother was born, things changed. Now my grandfather
plays the piano for me.

Curriculum Connections

Respond to this book by researching and playing the music that
accompanied the silent movies, early Broadway shows such as Ziegfield's
Follies, vaudeville shows, and musical comedies. Check your school,
public, or state university library collections for the music and videos. Two
videos to consider are *Scott Joplin*, which tells the story of the African
American musician, and *Vaudeville Videos*, which features a variety of
vaudeville acts and includes show business personalities such as W. C.
Fields, Sophie Tucker, and Eubie Blake. Be sure to preview the videos
before using them with the children. Have the children ask their grandparents if they have sheet music from the early 1900s through the

1930s that they could share with the class. A grandparent might even play the piano for your class.

Curtis, Gavin. **The Bat Boy & His Violin**. New York: Simon & Schuster Books for Young Readers, 1998. Unpaged. Illustrated by E. B. Lewis. $16.95. ISBN 0-689-80099-1.

■ **PICTURE BOOK—Fiction; African Americans**
■ **AGES 4–10**

Summary

When Reginald is not handling the bats for the Dukes, the worst team in the Negro National League in 1948, he plays his violin: Tchaikovsky, "Swan Lake," Mozart, Beethoven, Bach, the "Minute Waltz," and a Schubert sonata. Look for this book in the section "Sports" at the end of this chapter for full development of the booktalk, curriculum connections, and related books.

Karlins, Mark. **Music over Manhattan**. New York: Doubleday, 1998. 32p. Illustrated by Jack E. Davis. $15.95. ISBN 0-385-32225-9.

■ **PICTURE BOOK—Fiction**
■ **AGES 5–9**

Summary

Bernie lives in the shadow of his Cousin Herbert until Uncle Louie teaches Bernie how to play the trumpet. After a year of practicing, Bernie fills in for Uncle Louie's trumpet player at Cousin Hannah's wedding. When Bernie and the band play "Moonlight over Manhattan," swaying flowers, trembling oranges and bananas, and dancing wedding guests float into the air with the musicians, circle twice, drift across Manhattan, and flutter back to the ground in Brooklyn where they dance through the night.

Booktalk/Bookwalk/Read-Aloud

Either read aloud or retell the story while turning the pages and showing the pictures. What's that floating through the air? Why it looks like swaying flowers and trembling oranges and bananas drifting across Manhattan. And yes, there are the wedding guests and musicians fluttering to the ground in Brooklyn. Listen carefully. See what happens when Bernie and his band play "Moonlight over Manhattan."

Curriculum Connections

Play background music such as "Rhapsody in Blue" by George Gershwin. Brainstorm with the children what else might happen while Bernie and the band play "Moonlight Over Manhattan." Have children select or compose their own music then write and illustrate their own endings.

Koscielniak, Bruce. **The Story of the Incredible Orchestra**. Boston: Houghton Mifflin, 2000. Unpaged. $15.00. ISBN 0-395-96052-5.

■ **PICTURE BOOK—Nonfiction**
■ **AGES 5 and up**

Summary

Cartoon-like illustrations with labels and text introduce musical instruments of the orchestra (strings, woodwinds, brass, and percussion), beginning with those that predate the orchestra. The story of the orchestra and its instruments begins in the early 1600s with Gabrieli's Sacrae Symphoniae, continues through the baroque period of 1600–1750, into the classical period of 1750–1820, through the romantic period of 1820–1910, and concludes with the new sounds produced from the early 1900s to the present. Musicians are introduced along with evolving instruments and music.

Booktalk/Bookwalk

Do you play a musical instrument? Would you like to? Did you know that tooters, strings, and beaters are the three kinds of musical instruments? Did you know that once upon a time, the trombone was called a sackbut? Musical instruments have undergone many changes.

Today computer software will create music for you and synthesizers will modify and combine sounds. Take a look at the pictures in this book. See how musical instruments have changed and developed from before the 1600s to the present day.

Curriculum Connections

This book is a natural selection to use when introducing musical instruments. Each two-page spread focuses on one aspect of the development of the orchestra with easy-to-read labels for each instrument. Select music to accompany the introduction of the instruments. Play music from the periods featured. Check the collections in your public or state university library for the music you want to use following the reading of the book.

McGill, Alice. **In the Hollow of Your Hand: Slave Lullabies.** Boston: Houghton Mifflin, 2000. Unpaged. Illustrated by Michael Cummings. $18.00. ISBN 0-395-85755-4.

■ **PICTURE BOOK—African American Lullabies**
■ **AGES 3 and up**

Summary

Alice McGill collected thirteen lullabies that had been passed down among her family, friends, and neighbors in Mary's Chapel, North Carolina. Each two-page spread includes a lullaby, a short annotation that tells something about the song's history and the person who shared it with the author, and an illustration. Each full-page illustration appears as a quilt block and includes a quilting pattern. Music for each of the lullabies appears at the end of the book. A compact disc of the lullabies is taped to the inside of the front cover.

Bookwalk

Introduce the book by showing the cover, reading the title, and telling children that the author collected the lullabies in the book from family, friends, and neighbors in her community. Turn the pages to name each lullaby and show the illustrations. Call attention to details of the quilt motifs in the illustrations that depict the lullaby. For example, the first lullaby is "Sumtimes I Rock My Baby" and the illustration shows a mother holding her baby. After walking through the book, invite the children to listen to the compact disc recording of the lullabies.

Curriculum Connections

Play the compact disc. Teach the children to sing the lullabies. Extend the book by having children collect lullabies or music that have won a place in the hearts of family, friends, and neighbors. Compile individual or group books of well-loved music. Illustrate the books with quilt block designs.

Related Books

Alice McGill is the author of *Molly Bannaky*, which is reviewed in Chapter 3, "Social Studies" in "Autobiographies and Biographies."

McMullan, Kate, and Jim McMullan. **Papa's Song**. New York: Farrar, Straus & Giroux, 2000. Unpaged. $15.00. ISBN 0-374-35732-3.

■ **PICTURE BOOK—Fiction**
■ **AGES 3–7**

Summary

Granny, Grandpa, and Mama Bear each sing a lullaby, but Baby Bear is still awake. Papa Bear takes Baby Bear downriver in the bear boat, and the sounds of nature soothe Baby Bear to sleep.

Booktalk/Read-Aloud

Baby Bear just can't get to sleep! Granny Bear tries a lullaby; Grandpa Bear tries too. Even Mama Bear can't get Baby Bear to sleep. Then Papa Bear has an idea. Will it work? (Read aloud and show the pictures.)

Curriculum Connections

Talk about and sing lullabies that the children know, such as "Brahms' Lullaby." Ask the children if they have ever had trouble going to sleep. What helps them? Use the lullabies sung by Granny, Grandpa, and Mama Bear as a model to create additional four-line lullabies to sing to Baby Bear. Create new lullabies from the sounds of nature that put Baby Bear to sleep. Have children listen to the sounds in their immediate environment. Discuss how they might create a lullaby.

Schwartz, Amy. **Old MacDonald.** New York: Scholastic Press, 1999. Unpaged. $15.95. ISBN 0-590-46189-3.

■ **PICTURE BOOK—Song**
■ **AGES 5–8**

Summary

Full-page, brightly colored, cartoon-like illustrations enliven this retelling of the song, "Old MacDonald Had a Farm." E-I-E-I-O and the sounds of each animal are set in contrasting colors. The song with music is printed on the last page. Pictures of each animal appear in clockwise order to form a page border that can be used to cue each verse of the song.

Read-Aloud

Do you know the song "Old MacDonald"? Have you ever read the story? Well, here it is. All the animals and even the tractor get involved in this silly book. (Read aloud and invite children to chime in on the repetitions of E-I-E-I-O and the sounds of each animal.)

Curriculum Connections

A natural extension of this book is to sing the song after reading aloud. Discuss musical rounds and what they are. What other rounds do children know?

Scruggs, Afi. **Jump Rope Magic.** New York: Blue Sky Press, 2000. Unpaged. Illustrated by David Diaz. $16.95. ISBN 0-590-69327-1.

■ **PICTURE BOOK—Music; Movement; Verse**
■ **AGES 5–8**

Summary

Vibrant illustrations augment an equally vibrant text that bounces and sings with the rhythm and the music of jump rope rhymes and the story of Shameka and her jump rope friends. Booktalk and curriculum connections are fully developed in Chapter 1, "Language Arts and Literature" in "Poetry."

Vagin, Vladimir. **Peter and the Wolf**. New York: Scholastic Press, 2000. Unpaged. $15.95. ISBN 0-590-38608-5.

- **PICTURE BOOK—Symphony**
- **AGES 3–8**

Summary

Peter's grandfather tells him to close the garden gate to keep out the wolf. But it is a beautiful morning and the bird is chirping in the meadow, so Peter forgets. He leaves the gate open as he goes out into the meadow followed by the duck. As Peter spots the cat creeping after the bird, Grandpapa calls Peter home to shut the gate, just before the wolf appears in the meadow. The wolf swallows the duck and begins to stalk the cat while Peter, who is watching, devises a plan to catch the wolf. As soon as Peter catches the wolf, the hunters appear. They are determined to shoot the wolf, but Peter pleads to take the wolf to the zoo. Then the wolf spits out the duck and everyone lives happily ever after. The book ends with two pages of musical scores depicting the characters and a third page telling about the composer Sergei Prokofiev.

Book Talk/Read-Aloud

What would you do if a wolf were to come into your backyard? Long ago, people were afraid of wolves because wolves ate their animals. (Read aloud and show the pictures.)

Curriculum Connections

Play a recording of "Peter and the Wolf" and discuss the composition. Do some musical instruments sound more like animals than others? Which ones?

Warner, Sunny. **Madison Finds a Line**. Boston: Houghton Mifflin, 1999. 31p. $15.00. ISBN 0-395-88508-6.

■ **PICTURE BOOK—Fiction**
■ **AGES 5–8**

Summary

Madison spots a piece of rope in her yard and decides to follow it. With her cat, she follows the line between the sheets hanging on the clothesline and steps into an adventure of rhythm, music, dance, and art. Folk art motifs embellish the rhythmic text that is written in verse.

Booktalk/Bookwalk

Put on your dancing shoes and take out your singing voice. Come along with Madison as she and her cat travel a line between the white curtain of sheets into an adventure of rhythm, music, dance, and art. Dance like a toreador, do the shimmy-shammy rag, sing with a jitterbug jazz band, and when it rains invite the bugs into your umbrella boat. When the rain ends and the rainbow appears, dance the line with a salsa beat. This is the magical adventure that starts when Madison spots a piece of rope in her backyard and decides to follow it. (While giving the booktalk, show the book, turn the pages, and call attention to the illustrations that feature a line that continually changes its shape. This is also a great book for read-alouds.)

Curriculum Connections

The text lends itself to a wide array of responses: music, rhythm, dance, drawing, patterns and designs, drama, or poetry. Select music or have children use rhythm instruments as background music for the toreador dance, shimmy-shammy rag, jitterbug jazz band, and dance to the salsa beat. Have children create a time line of events, then lay a clothesline along the floor, act out the events of the story, and do the dances along the clothesline/time line. Use the illustrations as a model to make patterns and designs using variations on a straight line. Encourage children to extend the story by adding to Madison's adventures. Use the book as a model for writing in verse.

Weatherford, Carole Boston. **The Sound That Jazz Makes**. New York: Walker, 2000. Unpaged. Illustrated by Eric Velasquez. $16.95. ISBN 0-8027-8720-7.

- **PICTURE BOOK—Nonfiction; African Americans**
- **AGES 7 and up**

Summary

The story of jazz, from its African origins to the music of today's boom box rapper, dances off the pages of four-line text illustrated with vibrant oil paintings. Readers will recognize and respond to the cadence and repetitive use of "this is" in the beginning of the four-line stanzas reminiscent of *The House That Jack Built*.

Booktalk/Read-Aloud

Jazz is cool! Meet Louis Armstrong, Duke Ellington, Cab Calloway, and other jazz musicians. Where does rap music come from? Come on along and listen to the story of jazz, which begins with its African origins and finds its way into the music of today's boom box. (The rhythmic, rhyming four-line text on each page is intended to be read aloud.)

Curriculum Connections

A natural response to this book would be to listen to recordings of early jazz musicians and contemporary hip-hop. Encourage children to select and even perform their hip-hop favorites. Show the video *Weston Woods Presents Duke Ellington the Piano Prince and His Orchestra* (Pinkney, Andrea Davis. *Weston Woods Presents Duke Ellington*. Produced by Top Dog Media, Inc. Directed by Ray Messacar. 15 min. Weston Woods, 2000. Videocassette), which was adapted from a children's book of the same name. (Be sure to preview the video before using it.) Finally, visit a Web site of jazz musicians such as Jazz Roots at http://www.jass.com.

Ziefert, Harriet. **Animal Music**. Boston: Houghton Mifflin, 1999. Unpaged. Illustrated by Donald Saaf. $15.00. ISBN 0-395-95294-8.

- **PICTURE BOOK—Concept Book**
- **AGES 3–7**

Summary

Mr. Lion's marching band and Mr. Sheep's dance band feature favorite animals playing musical instruments.

Booktalk/Read-Aloud

Here comes Mr. Lion's marching band. What a ruckus they make! Then Mr. Sheep's dance band tries to outdo them. How many animals play how many instruments? Look inside. (Read aloud and show the pictures.)

Curriculum Connections

Have children act out the story with a variety of rhythm bands or musical instruments used in the book.

DANCE

Edwards, Pamela Duncan. **Honk! The Story of a Prima Swanerina.** Westport, CT: Hyperion Press, 1998. 32p. Illustrated by Henry Cole. $14.95. ISBN 0-7868-0435-1.

∎ **PICTURE BOOK—Fiction**
∎ **AGES 5–8**

Summary

Mimi, the swan, follows a ballerina through the stage door and onto the stage of the Paris Opera House. She is such a success that the manager invites Mimi to return for the next day's performance.

Booktalk/Read-Aloud

Mimi the swan has a dancing heart, but the manager says, "No birds allowed in the Opera House!" Poor Mimi's heart is broken. Mimi loves the ballet. After looking through the windows of the Paris Opera House and seeing the dancers perform, she practices every day. One day when one of the ballerinas arrives late, Mimi follows her through the stage door and right onto the stage. Can you imagine what happens then?

Curriculum Connections

Read aloud and show the pictures. For dramatic effects, softly play Tchaikovsky's "Swan Lake" as background music. Talk about ballet and what it is. Does anyone take ballet lessons? (Children who are or have taken ballet lessons may be willing to demonstrate dance steps or do a simple dance for the group.) Have any of you ever seen ballet on TV or onstage? Did you like it? Why or why not?

Freschet, Gina. **Naty's Parade**. New York: Farrar, Straus & Giroux, 2000. Unpaged. $16.00. ISBN 0-374-35500-2.

- ■ **PICTURE BOOK—Fiction; Hispanic; Bilingual/ESOL**
- ■ **AGES 5–8**

Summary

Naty, her father, and a neighbor are going to town to celebrate Guelaguetza, a festival of folkloric dances held in Oaxaca, Mexico, on the last two Mondays of July. For the first time, Naty will march in the parade as a dancing mouse with the puppet people. But she drops her whistle, gets lost, and must find her way back to Papa.

Booktalk

Oops! As Naty spins around as a dancing mouse, she drops the little whistle that Papa gave her. It tumbles down the alley, and of course, she has to go after it. Naty finds her whistle but loses the parade. Now how will she find her way back to the parade and Papa?

Curriculum Connections

Look for and play audio or videotapes of folkloric music and dance. Songs and music of the Guelaguetza Festival of Oaxaca can be found on the compact discs, *La Guelaguetza la musica autentica del espectaculo folklorico mas importante de America* (1998, 1996. 2 compact discs). The videos, *Folklorico*, vol. 1 (59 min. 1999. Video-cassette) and vol. 2 (53 min. 1999. Videocassette) demonstrate and teach Mexican folk dances. Traditional costumes, choreography, costume designs, and regional histories are included in the accompanying booklets. You should be able to find the tapes and compact discs in the collections at your public library or state university library. Use this book with a study of folk dances, in particular, the folkloric dances of Oaxaca, Mexico. What are some of the instruments used in the parade? See if you can find a musician to visit the class and demonstrate some instruments, or have children draw pictures of instruments and dancers. Encourage children to choreograph and present a dance to depict Naty's dancing in the parade, getting lost, and finding her way back to the parade. Invite a dancer from your community or a parent who is a dancer to help you.

Related Books

A Spanish version of this book is also available. Freschet, Gina. *La procession de Naty*. New York: Farrar, Straus & Giroux, 2000. $16.00. ISBN 0-374-36136-3.

Staples, Suzanne Fisher. **Shiva's Fire**. New York: Farrar, Straus & Giroux, 2000. 276p. $17.00. ISBN 0-374-36824-4.

■ **CHAPTER BOOK—Fiction; Asian Indian; Hindu**
■ **AGES 10–14**

Summary

Parvati is born in India on the same day that the cyclone destroys the village and kills her father. So villagers look upon her with suspicion, believing that she is endowed with supernatural powers. Then the Guru from the city of Madras recognizes Parvati's gift for dancing. He invites her to attend the school of Indian classical dance in Madras where Parvati quickly becomes the most talented dancer in all of India. When the Maharaja invites Parvati to dance for him, she meets and falls in love with the Maharaja's son, and has to choose between her desire to dance and her love for the young man.

Booktalk

Parvati is the most talented dancer in all of India. She loves to dance, but she also loves the Maharaja's son. Now she must choose. Which will it be—the dance or the Maharaja's son?

Curriculum Connections

Two videos, *Visions and Sounds of Indian Classical Dance* (Srirama, Malini, Tom Hemingway, K. S. Sridhar, and Lisa D. Hurwitz. *Visions and Sounds of Indian Classical Dance*. Produced by Malini Srirama. Directed by K. S. Sridhar and Lisa D. Hurwitz. 23 min. 1990. Videocassette), which demonstrates Indian classical dancing, and *Adrienne Cherie Interprets Dances of India* (Cherie, Adrienne. *Adrienne Cherie Interprets Dances of India*. Produced by Adrienne Cherie. Directed by Louis Zweier. 35 min. 1988. Videocassette), which interprets dances of India, may be used to introduce the book or as a follow-up activity. (Be sure to preview the videos before showing them.)

DRAMA

Hamilton, Virginia. **The Girl Who Spun Gold.** New York: Blue Sky Press, 2000. Unpaged. Illustrated by Leo Dillon and Diane Dillon. $16.95. ISBN 0-590-47378-6.

- ■ **PICTURE BOOK: Multicultural; West Indies**
- ■ **AGES 5–8**

Summary

This retelling of the West Indian variant on Rumplestiltskin reflects the lilting West Indian speech pattern. Illustrations make lavish use of gold leaf and repetitive patterns and designs.

Booktalk/Read-Aloud

It all started when Mama lied to Big King by telling him that her daughter, Quashiba, could spin an entire field into gold. So Big King and Quashiba were quickly married. Then Big King told his new Queen that she must spin three rooms full of gold. Lit'mahn, who was hiding in the bushes when Mama lied to Big King, came floating through the window to make a bargain with Queenie Quashie. He agreed to spin the gold, but she must guess his name. If she couldn't guess his name, he would carry her off to live with him. Lit'mahn spun the gold and Queenie Quashie guessed Septimus, Obidiah, Jemajama. At each name, Lit'mahn laughed and shouted "No-a!" Then she guessed Nicholas, Nehemiah, and Nebercouldgethim. Again Lit'mahn laughed and shouted

"No-a!" Whatever was Queenie Quashie to do? How would she ever discover Lit'mahn's name?

Curriculum Connections

The lilting language used in the text begs to be read aloud and to be performed. Assign roles: Big King, Mama, Quashiba, Lit'mahn, Everybody, and Narrator. Have students develop a readers' theater script and perform for the whole class. Use the repetitive patterns and designs in the illustrations as models for the children's artwork. Have children paint new illustrations using repetitive patterns and designs as did the Dillons.

Olaleye, Isaac O. **In the Rainfield: Who Is the Greatest?** New York: Blue Sky Press, 2000. Unpaged. Illustrated by Ann Grifalconi. $15.95. ISBN 0-590-48363-3.

■ **PICTURE BOOK—Nigeria**
■ **AGES 4–9**

Summary

This retelling of a Nigerian folktale is illustrated with vibrant collages. Wind, Rain, and Fire argue about which is the greatest. Wind blows; Fire rages. When Fire refuses to stop, Wind tries to blow it out but only makes it stronger. Rain drips gently but steadily and puts out the raging Fire, thereby proving that "the gentlest is the greatest."

Booktalk

Who do you think is greatest—Wind, Fire, or Rain? Well, did you know that once upon a time Wind, Fire, and Rain had an argument over who was the most powerful? Who do you think won the argument?

Curriculum Connections

Retell the story using creative dramatics. Select to celebrate Black History Month.

SPORTS

Christopher, Matt. **Prime-Time Pitcher**. Boston: Little, Brown, 1998. 138p. $3.95. ISBN 0-316-14213-1.

■ **CHAPTER BOOK—Fiction**
■ **AGES 8–12**

Summary

Koby pitches his team into a winning streak, but then discovers that his team and classmates are turning away from him. It is in the final game of the conference championship that Koby discovers how much he depends on the support and encouragement of his teammates. The brisk pacing of this action story will appeal to young readers.

Booktalk

With his catcher, Tug, calling the signals and his teammates supporting and encouraging him and each other, Koby pitches his team into a winning streak. Suddenly, Koby finds himself thrust into the center of attention when the Channel 5 Evening News team selects him as the focus of a documentary on middle school athletics. Now he is a superstar, but his team and classmates are turning away from him. All Koby had wanted was to pull the Cardinals out of the slump that they had been in for several years. What went wrong?

Curriculum Connections

Excerpts from the school paper, *The Megaphone*, are interspersed throughout this book. Each excerpt includes "Sports Shorts" Trivia Questions. Encourage children to write their own "Sports Shorts" Trivia Questions. Extend the activity by encouraging children to develop a "Sports Shorts" board game. Construct math problems with scores and batting averages.

Related Books

Prime-Time Pitcher is the fifty-ninth book in a series of sports books about baseball, basketball, football, soccer, hockey, skateboarding, dirt biking, swimming, snowboarding, and roller hockey by Matt Christopher. Matt Christopher has also written biographies about Andre

Agassi, Wayne Gretzky, Ken Griffey Jr., Grant Hill, Greg Maddux, Randy Johnson, Michael Jordan, Hakeem Olajuwon, Emmitt Smith, Mo Vaughn, Tiger Woods, and Steve Young. All titles are listed in the back of the book.

Curtis, Gavin. **The Bat Boy & His Violin.** New York: Simon & Schuster Books for Young Readers, 1998. Unpaged. Illustrated by E. B. Lewis. $16.95. ISBN 0-689-80099-1.

■ **PICTURE BOOK—Fiction; African Americans**
■ **AGES 4–10**

Summary

When Reginald is not handling the bats for the Dukes, the worst team in the Negro National League in 1948, he plays his violin: Tchaikovsky, "Swan Lake," Mozart, Beethoven, Bach, the "Minute Waltz," and a Schubert sonata.

Booktalk

The Dukes are the worst baseball team in the Negro National League. Reginald's father manages the Dukes and he wants Reginald to become a baseball player. But Reginald wants to play his violin with a famous orchestra. Reginald is practicing for his violin recital that is only a month away when Papa comes home and says that the Dukes need a batboy. But Reginald needs to practice for his recital. Should he give up the violin to make his father happy?

Curriculum Connections

This book lends itself to a discussion of team spirit and family ties. Select and play recordings of the violin music and composers that Reginald practiced.

Related Books

Fair Ball! 14 Great Stars from Baseball's Negro Leagues, reviewed at the end of this section, "Sports," introduces readers to fourteen baseball players from the Negro Leagues. *The Journal of Biddy Owens: The Negro Leagues* by Walter Dean Meyers is one of the Dear America: My Name

Is America Series. It tells the story of Biddy Owens who was batboy for the Birmingham Black Barons, one of the best teams in the Negro League.

Forsyth, C. A. **Hockey Heat Wave**. Toronto: James Lorimer, 1998. 79p. $5.50. ISBN 1-55028-619-6.

■ **CHAPTER BOOK—Fiction**
■ **AGES 8–13**

Summary

Thirteen-year-old Mitch and his best friend Zack spend two weeks at hockey camp in northern Ontario with thirty-eight of the best hockey players in Ontario. Of the forty boys at camp, only twenty-five will be chosen for the all-star team. From the beginning things go wrong. Then Zack injures his foot and refuses to tell anyone except Mitch.

Booktalk

I thought two weeks at hockey camp with my best friend, Zack, and thirty-eight of the best hockey players in Ontario was going to be great! Then we learned that only twenty-five of us would be selected for the all-star team. The next thing you know, Zack cut his foot badly—and he wouldn't let us tell anyone. When he started running a temperature and got delirious, we knew we had to get him to a hospital. But how could we do that without telling? And how was he going to make the all-star team if he couldn't skate? Would I be able to make the all-star team without Zack? Would I even want to without Zack?

Curriculum Connections

This is a fast-paced, suspenseful story. Each of the thirteen chapters begins with three paragraphs that set the tone for the remainder of the chapter. Have students read the first three paragraphs, predict what will happen, and then read the chapter to confirm their predictions. Create a Sample/Predict/Confirm Story Chart. See Appendix A for a sample.

McCully, Emily Arnold. **Mouse Practice**. New York: Arthur A. Levine Books, 1999. Unpaged. $15.95. ISBN 0-590-68220-2.

■ **PICTURE BOOK—Fiction**
■ **AGES 3–7**

Summary

Monk the mouse wants to learn how to play baseball. His parents who are musicians try to help, even though they know very little about baseball. With a little help from his parents and a lot of practice, Monk is accepted on the neighborhood team.

Booktalk

Monk couldn't catch, couldn't throw, and couldn't hit the ball. The big kids weren't mad at him. They just felt sorry for him. "Come back when you're bigger," they said. Monk the mouse really, really wanted to learn how to play baseball. His parents tried to help him, but they were musicians and knew very little about baseball. Guess how Monk solves his problem and how the team ends up with their own band.

Curriculum Connections

Monk was a creative problem solver. He needed a target, and he needed to practice batting and catching without a pitcher. Read aloud. Pause to ask the children, "What would you do?" after the big kids felt sorry for Monk, when he needed a target, and when he needed to practice batting and catching.

Walters, Eric. **Three on Three**. Custer, WA: Orca, 2000. 96p. $3.99. ISBN 1-55143-170-X.

■ **CHAPTER BOOK—Fiction**
■ **AGES 8–11**

Summary

Nick and Kia learn about team-man-ship when Marcus agrees to play on their team in the Three-on-Three Basketball Tournament.

Booktalk

Nick and Kia want to enter the Three-on-Three Basketball Tournament. They also want to win. Although they are the best third-grade basketball players in the school, the only way they can win against the fourth- and fifth-graders is to have Marcus, the best fifth-grade player, on their team. But all of the fifth-graders, and fourth-graders also, want Marcus to play on their teams. So why would Marcus want to play with the little kids? How can Nick and Kia talk Marcus into playing on their team?

Curriculum Connections

Nick, Kia, and Marcus learn that becoming a winning team is more than putting three good players on the same team. Instead of each player being the best, they learn to play together as a team. Reread Chapter 11 and have the children discuss what it means to play as a team. Encourage them to look for applications in their own lives.

Winter, Jonah. **Fair Ball! 14 Great Stars from Baseball's Negro Leagues**. New York: Scholastic Press, 1999. Unpaged. $15.95. ISBN 0-590-39464-9.

- ■ **PICTURE BOOK—Nonfiction; Multicultural;**
  African Americans
- ■ **AGES 7 and up**

Summary

A two-page spread with text and a picture on opposite pages introduces readers to fourteen star baseball players from the Negro Leagues. Black men formed their own leagues because they were not allowed to play in the major leagues. The book concludes with the author's pick of all-star teams made up of black and white players for the American and National Leagues. The teams are made up of white and black players.

Booktalk

Who hit more home runs than Babe Ruth? Josh Gibson, that's who! Who was the fastest baseball player, the greatest, the scariest, or the smartest? Black baseball players, who played in the Negro Leagues, earned those titles because they were not allowed to play in the major leagues. The best left-handed pitcher, the greatest power-hitter, the best catcher, and the best first baseman were also black baseball players. Find out more about fourteen great baseball players from the Negro Leagues.

Curriculum Connections

Baseball stars of the Negro Leagues went unrecognized for decades. Using this book as a reference, give them the recognition they deserve by creating news stories for the newspaper, radio, and television. Design and make baseball cards for the players. Select your own all-star teams of black and white players.

Related Books

The Bat Boy & His Violin, reviewed above, is a story about a boy who serves as batboy for the Dukes, the worst team in the Negro National League. *The Journal of Biddy Owens: The Negro Leagues* by Walter Dean Meyers is one of the Dear America: My Name Is America Series. It tells the story of Biddy Owens who was batboy for the Birmingham Black Barons, one of the best teams in the Negro League.

Appendix A: Graphic Organizers

- Character Web

- Character Wheel

- Fish Bone

- Parallel Story Chart

- Problem-Solving Chart

- Sample/Predict/Confirm Story Chart

- Semantic Feature Analysis Chart

- Story Map Based on Setting

- Time Line

- Venn Diagram

Character Web for

_____

(name of book)

DIRECTIONS

1. Draw and/or name a character in the center circle.

2. Write three character traits in the surrounding rectangles.

3. Find examples from the book that tell specifically what this character did or said that supports the traits you picked. Write these in the ovals.

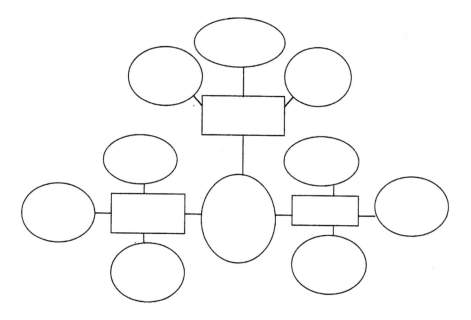

Character Wheel

DIRECTIONS

1. Read a biography or fictional story, paying careful attention to the personality and actions of the main character.

2. When you have finished, list character traits of the main character.

3. Make your own character wheel using the wheel below.

   - Print the name of the character and the book's title and author in the center.

   - Put a character trait in each spoke of the wheel.

   - Include pictures, notes, or quotes from the book to explain the character's actions, to tell more about a particular trait, or just to add interest.

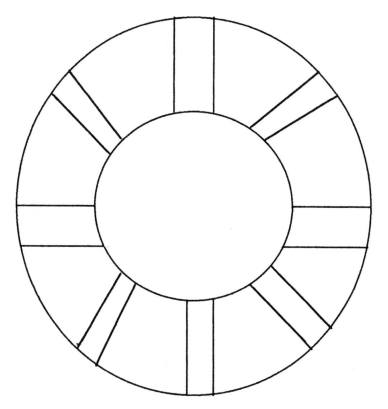

Fish Bone

The fish bone can be used for a variety of purposes such as identifying cause and effect, identifying problems and solutions, or a time line with events. Write one set of information such as causes on the upper lines. Write a second set of information such as effects on the lower lines.

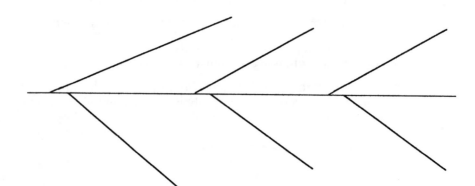

Parallel Story Chart for
Monk Camps Out

On the chart, list what Monk did and what his parents did at each action event in the story.

Events	Monk	Parents
Beginning	Decides to camp out	Think he'll change his mind
Action event	Makes a tent	Help him a little
Action event	Eats camp grub	Eat a quiet dinner
Action event	Sun goes down	Lights turned off
Action event	Alone in the quiet	Go out to give a good night hug
Action event	Awakens and wants mitt	Fall asleep in chairs then awaken
Action event	Goes in front door for mitt	Go out back door to check on him
Action event	Falls asleep in Mom's chair	Fall asleep outside tent
Conclusion	Awakens and runs out	Awaken and run in

Problem-Solving Chart for
Dear Mrs. Ryan, You're
Ruining My Life

On the chart, identify the person, problems, solutions, and problem-solving strategies.

Person	Problem	Solution	Strategies
Harvey	Mom writes about Harvey	Boyfriend for Mom	Identify boyfriend Arrange meeting
	Mom dates principal	Deny Avoid Undo relationship Accept relationship	Lie to friends Lie to mother Annoy boyfriend

Sample/Predict/Confirm Story Chart

On the chart list students' predictions (what students think will happen) for each chapter. After students have read the chapter list students' confirmations (what actually happened).

Chapters	Predictions (What I Think Will Happen)	Confirmations (What Actually Happened)
Chapter 1		
Chapter 2		
Chapter 3		
Chapter 4		
Chapter 5		
Chapter 6		
Chapter 7		
Chapter 8		
Chapter 9		
Chapter 10		
Chapter 11		
Chapter 12		
Chapter 13		

Semantic Feature Analysis Chart

Use the chart to compare multiple features of three or more things.

DIRECTIONS

1. Identify features across the top.

2. Identify items down the side.

3. In each column indicate whether or not the item possesses the identified feature.

4. Use a coding system such as + or -, yes or no, or smiling or frowning face.

Items	Feature	Feature	Feature	Feature
	+	−	+	+
	−	−	+	−
	−	+	+	−
	+	+	−	+

Story Map Based on Setting for
The Red Bandanna

On the chart, list the settings with the events and characters that occurred in the settings.

Settings	Events	Characters
Woodshed	Coyote pups were born.	Shadow
Fence	Shadow led Jake to Ten.	Shadow, Jake, Ten
Jake's kitchen	Ten was dropper fed by Jake's mother.	Ten, Jake's mother
Jake's bedroom	Shadow howled for Ten.	Shadow, Jake, Ten
Jake's yard	Griff Webster left a dead calf.	Griff Webster, Calf, Jake
Griff Webster's lane	Griff Webster had a change of heart.	Griff Webster, Ten, Jake

Time Line

On the chart list the dates and events that occurred on those dates.

Dates	Events

Venn Diagram

- Use the Venn Diagram to compare and contrast likenesses and differences.

- List differences in outer portions of circles.

- List likenesses in inner overlapping portion of circles.

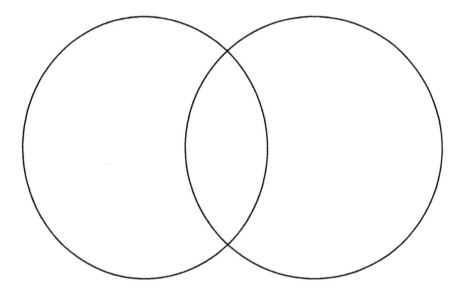

Appendix B:
Directions and Recipes

- Salt Dough Mixture

- Split-Twig Animal Figures

Salt Dough Mixture

INGREDIENTS

1 part salt
1 part non-self-rising flour
2/3 part water
Food coloring or tempera paint

DIRECTIONS

1. Mix flour and salt thoroughly.

2. Add water to consistency of thick icing.

3. Stir thoroughly.

4. Add food coloring before molding or mold and paint when dry.

5. Build up elevations in layers. Let each layer dry before applying the next.

6. Allow one to two days for drying.

Split-Twig Animal Figures

MATERIALS

3-foot length of commercial basketry reed or
Wrapped wire or cottonwood twigs

DIRECTIONS

1. Fold the reed in half. Pinch tightly.

2. Approximately one inch from the folded end of the reed, bend the reed down at a 90-degree angle to make the hind legs.

3. Approximately one-and-a-half inches from the new fold, bend the reed down at a 90-degree angle, then bend it up again to make the front legs.

4. Form the body by bending the reed around the outside of the legs about four times.

5. Form the head and neck by bending the tall reed about one inch above the body and again about one-half inch from the first bend.

6. Bring the reed down one side; bend it around the belly and up alongside the neck once again.

7. Fold the reed over the head and wrap it four or five times around the neck.

8. When you have used most of the reed, tuck in the loose end, or squeeze it tightly against the body of the figure.

Author/Title Index

Subject Index